DRAGONS VS WOLVES

FALLEN STAR

To Kev, Lyn and Andy, the cubs I grew up with—G.D.

Scholastic Australia
An imprint of Scholastic Australia Pty Limited
PO Box 579 Gosford NSW 2250
ABN 11 000 614 577
www.scholastic.com.au

Part of the Scholastic Group
Sydney • Auckland • New York • Toronto • London • Mexico City •
New Delhi • Hong Kong • Buenos Aires • Puerto Rico

Published by Scholastic Australia in 2024.

Cover and internals illustrations by Mariano Epelbaum.

Book design by Chad Mitchell.

NATIONAL LIBRARY OF AUSTRALIA

A catalogue record for this book is available from the National Library of Australia

ISBN: 978-93-5954-815-9

This Reprint Edition: March 2026
Printed In India at Shiv Shakti Printing and Trading Co., Haryana

Typeset in Adobe Garamond Pro.

GLENN DAKIN

DRAGONS VS WOLVES

FALLEN STAR

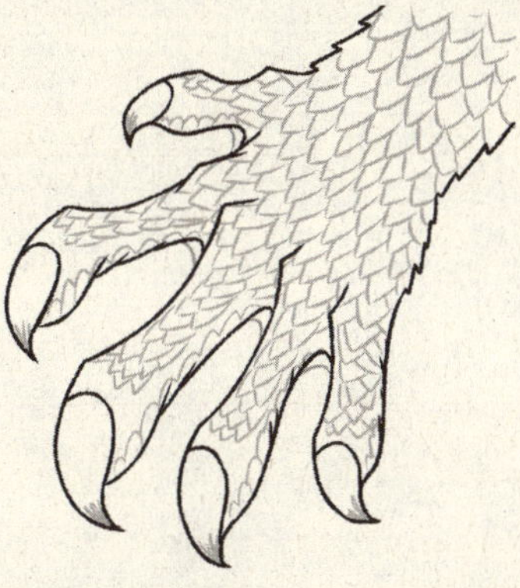

A Scholastic Australia Book

CONTENTS

Last Rock
Barren Isles
Spook Bay
Hunter's Reach
Frost Forest
Bear River
Rushing Waters
Pine Top
Spiral Cave
Long Creek
Shooting Star
(Ungoria)
Rana & Fenn Exile Journey

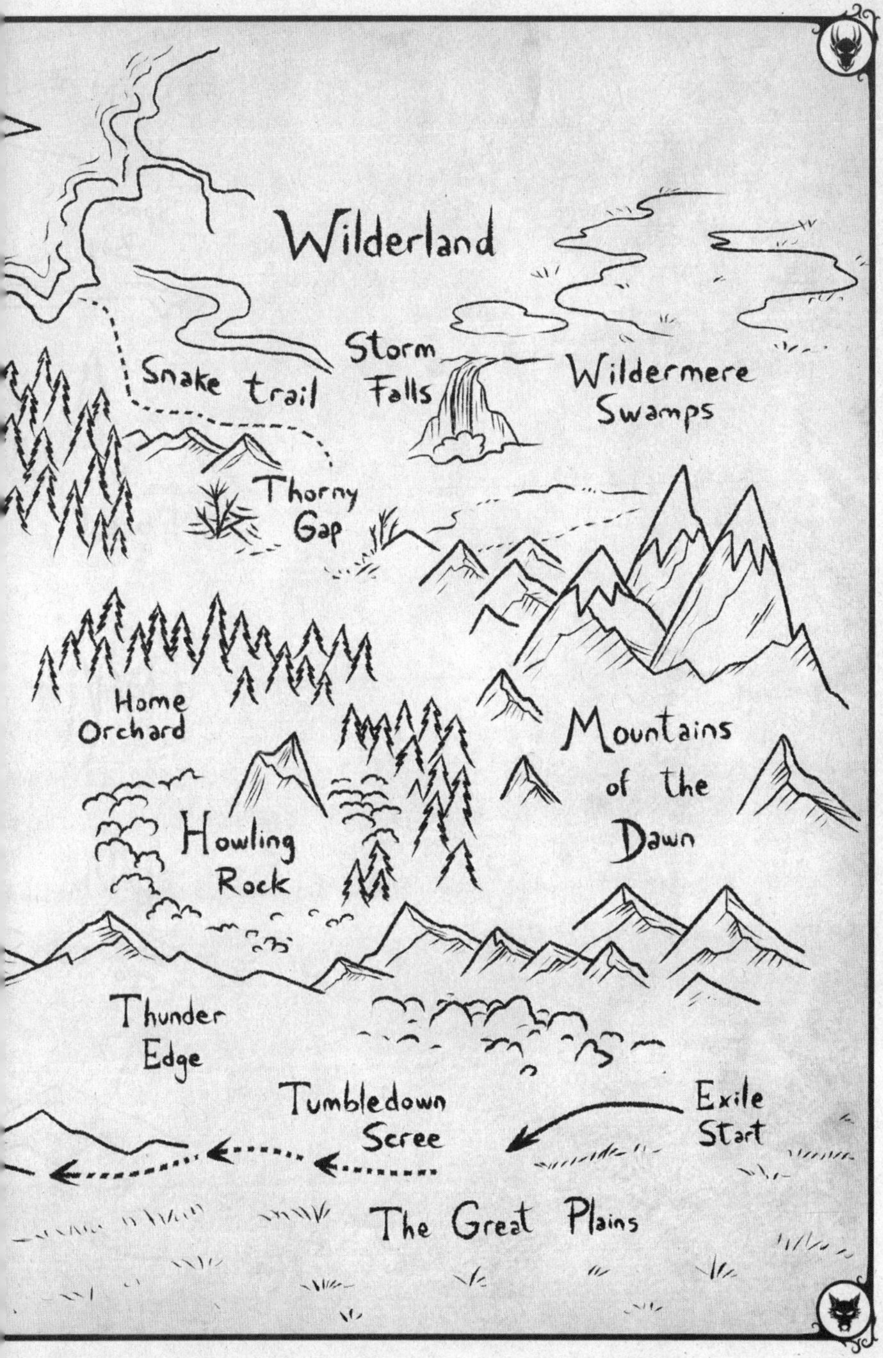
Wilderland
Snake trail
Storm Falls
Wildermere Swamps
Thorny Gap
Home Orchard
Mountains of the Dawn
Howling Rock
Thunder Edge
Tumbledown Scree
Exile Start
The Great Plains

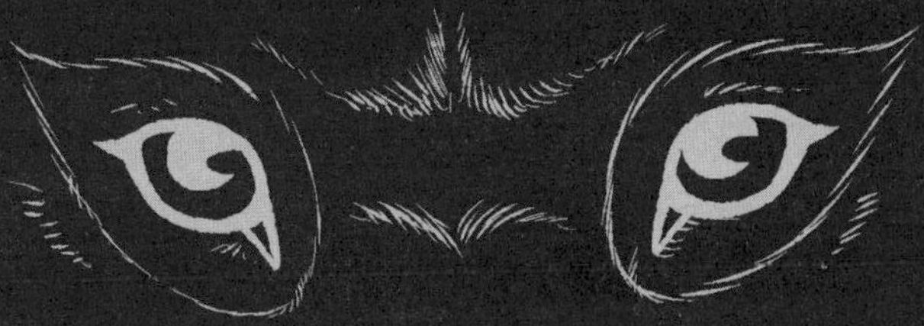

In the Beginning Time, a Great Darkness lay on the world.

From that shadow was made the First Wolf, Fera.

The First Wolf ate the Great Darkness and the sun rose.

It spread its rays, and the Eternal Forest appeared.

The sun said to Fera, 'All this land is for you and

your children to roam free.'

But the sun discovered it could not spread light

without making shadows.

And in the shadows lay the dragons.

Frost
Forest
Bear River
Rushing
Waters
Pine
Top
Long Creek

Part One:

The Great Pack

CHAPTER 1

It was the most terrifying thing Rana had ever seen in her life. And it was coming straight at her.

'Get back,' roared Darkmane. 'Way back!'

The grizzly kept coming. Rana leapt behind the antlers of the dead elk that lay sprawled in the bracken. This was what the bear was really after.

'Stay with Fenn,' growled their mother. She had been trying to keep her two young wolves out of trouble in the shadow of the carcass.

Rana and Fenn, the only yearlings in the party, slunk back and forth behind the body of the elk. Darkmane stood guard in front of it, baring his teeth in a ferocious growl.

Looming before them was the vast mound of muscle and reeking fur of an angry grizzly. Its enormous, shaggy head had a battered look, a scar running below one half-closed eye. A blood-curdling roar sent tremors through Rana's body, making her shiver to the silvery tips of her ears.

'This was such a great idea of yours,' Fenn said to her, sarcastically. He was leaping about, trying to look fierce. '"Let us go on the patrol," you said! "What could possibly happen?" you said.'

'You're choosing *now* to give me a hard time?' asked Rana. 'When I've got a grizzly in my face?'

Darkmane was their father and the leader of the Starlight wolf pack. He had allowed the young wolves to join a routine patrol down Long Creek. On their way back, they had discovered the body of an elk, slumped among the bracken. This was a rare bounty and would feed them for days. The fastest wolf in their patrol, Lightfoot, had gone to fetch the rest of the pack. The others, including Rana, had remained to guard the dead elk. Then the grizzly had shown up.

Of course, Rana had been taught about protecting a carcass from other predators. *Even weak animals can be part of a show of strength if they know how to act*, her father had said. Rana had a feeling she didn't know how to act. She was slightly smaller than most wolves of her age, her fur a pale, silvery gray. There was little about her that inspired fear in an enemy.

The big bear shambled another step or two towards the elk. Gripper, Darkmane's lieutenant, rushed at it, feigning an attack, then pulling away. A deadly paw just missed his head.

'Easy,' said Darkmane. 'I don't want to lose anywolf here.'

Two more of the older wolves stood shoulder to shoulder with Darkmane, snarling. The bear wavered, seeming uncertain of its next move. Rana noticed a loose, floppy quality to its skin. It was patchy too. Its face wore a wounded look, almost of sorrow.

It's an old one, she thought. *We might stand a chance.*

But at stake was a large, tasty elk. Very fresh. No-one was giving up on it easily. A kind of stand-off seemed to have set in.

'Keep it cool, we've got this,' growled Darkmane. Suddenly, the bear flung itself forward at the carcass. The older wolves yelped, parted and scattered. Rana and Fenn leapt away.

'Don't lose it, don't lose it!' roared Darkmane, rushing back at the bear and sinking a bite into its hind leg. A great paw smacked him away, sending him rolling into the dirt.

'Darkmane!' yelped Gripper.

The chief wolf struggled back to his feet, groggy but unhurt. The grizzly took a determined step forward. Then another. Now it was the wolves' turn to waver. Gripper retreated, barking without conviction. Rana and Fenn huddled a bit lower behind the antlers. Their mother stepped in front of them and joined in the uncertain growling.

A crashing noise in the forest behind them made Rana whip round. More danger?

A loud baying filled the air. Through the trees erupted a whole pack of wolves, their jaws wide, their eyes alight.

The grizzly stumbled back, its old head slowly turning this way and that as it took in the odds. A dark-brown wolf with a golden flash along her back rushed to Darkmane's side. Rana's heart leapt. It was Sunstreak from their sister-pack.

'That's Greyface, the Old Man of the Woods!' cried Sunstreak. 'We can take him!'

Rana peered through the twisted antlers and watched the wolves leap and snap at the grizzly. Now, the battle was truly on. Gripper whined as a claw shredded one of his ears. Darkmane landed a bite on the grizzly's lower flank. Greyface bellowed and heaved up his claws and the attackers all danced away. Fenn leapt up and bared his teeth in a snarl as the bear lumbered once more towards the prize. Rana's mother shoved her away from the carcass.

And I don't even like elk, thought Rana.

Before Greyface could settle on the body, Gripper and Sunstreak snapped savagely at his neck, forcing him to retreat.

Now, more wolves arrived, stragglers from Sunstreak's pack. At speed, they circled the bear. It turned this way and that, confused, claws flailing at nothing. Rana crept towards the action, shielded by her mother. Darkmane leapt up at the bear's back, with Gripper snapping at his side. With a final, sad look at the dead elk, Greyface suddenly made up his mind. He turned away.

'He's going!' Fenn cried. Rana sensed his relief.

The older wolves followed the grizzly like a flowing wave of fur. It vanished into the timber at astonishing speed. Rana watched with a strange feeling in her heart. It seemed almost unfair on the Old Man of the Woods.

'Will they kill him?' Rana asked her mother.

Ayala gave a wry grin. 'Our kind do kill bears from time to time,' she said. 'But not this one, I reckon. He's given up on this feast, that's the main thing.'

In a short while, the pursuers abandoned the chase and returned to the carcass. There was no bear-kill, but they had their victory.

It was party time.

The sun had dropped behind the mountains and shadows now gathered under the trees. Sunstreak's pack had joined Darkmane's and the clearing around the elk carcass was full of life and chatter. Everyone was having fun ripping at the carcass and telling each other how brave and snarly they were. Scars and scratches were compared, and friendly fights were breaking out here and there. Rana padded quietly around the edge of the celebrations—she had seen enough fighting for one day.

'I showed him I wasn't scared,' said Fenn. 'I threatened him, like this, and this, and this!' He acted out a series of snapping motions with his jaws at an imaginary grizzly. Rana, listening from a distance, rolled her eyes to the sky.

'What about Rana?' asked Ela. A yearling like Rana, she loved an audience and always made the most of a visit from the Sundown pack. She tossed her snow-white mane and narrowed her eyes. 'I don't hear much of Rana's heroics. But I heard she was there.'

'Oh yes,' said Fenn, 'Rana was there. Terrified, of course! I protected her, Ela, don't worry about that!'

'I *wasn't* worried about that, actually,' Ela replied, with a small yawn. 'I mean, we all know how fast Rana is—to find a hiding place, that is.' A couple of the Sundown wolves sniggered.

'That's her, alright,' said Fenn. 'I wasn't frightened, of course,' he added. 'Actually, I have a sort of natural sense for danger. My dad calls it the Scent. And this time I just wasn't feeling it. I knew we'd come out on top . . .'

Rana groaned inwardly. Fenn was boasting about his so-called abilities, as usual. And Ela was on her case, as ever. Big occasions always brought the worst out in her pack. Wolves became more, well . . . *wolvish* when they got together in numbers.

She padded off to find Karla. The old storyteller would be with the newest cubs.

From a distance, she could see Karla curled up on a cosy bed of fern, on the edge of the clearing. Three little cubs lay peering up at her. Rana decided to sneak round the back so she could overhear the stories.

Darkmane stood in her way.

'You could have done better today, Rana,' he said. 'You didn't do much more than watch. And you probably had your eyes closed.'

Rana lowered her body in the suitable submissive pose. She didn't meet his gaze.

'I'm only a—'

'A yearling, yes, but so is Fenn, and he was leaping around, distracting the grizzly, making his presence felt. A show of strength is what it's all about. Remember that.'

'Yes, Dad.'

Rana slunk away. Scent or no scent, Fenn had been as scared as her. Still, what her father had said was true. She had been pretty useless. Feeling low, she weaved her way through the saplings on the edge of the clearing to where old Karla was holding court.

Rana stopped to admire the way the old she-wolf had the little cubs gazing up at her with awe as she told her tales. Rana would love to inspire a feeling like that. Instead, she seemed to attract criticism like flies on a dead rat.

'. . . so the three little pups ate the big tasty bison, and they all lived happily ever after,' crooned Karla. Rana was sorry she had missed the story—*The Big Tasty Bison* was one of her favourites. She settled down in the ferns behind them.

'Tell it again!' begged a cub.

'Tell us the bit about his soft, chewy ears,' pleaded another.

'Maybe another time.' Karla smiled. 'Now run along, your families will be missing you.'

The little cubs scampered off, jumping on top of each other and rolling in the grass. From the carcass party, whoops and howls filled the air. Twilight was descending, making the sky behind the trees a deep blue. A thin, new moon had risen above the mountains to the east.

'It's a big night,' said Karla. 'The pack driving off a grizzly! A fresh elk to feast on. Fera—the First Wolf—is smiling on us.'

Rana crept in closer to her, taking the place of the departed cubs. 'She's not smiling on me.' She sighed.

'You've had a hard day,' said the old wolf. 'And your first big adventure.'

'Well, you wouldn't think so,' said Rana, 'from the way I keep getting told off.'

More howls of laughter drifted across the clearing, with the clear sounds of Fenn whooping away.

'Fenn was just as scared as I was,' she said. 'But because of his "show of strength", he comes out of it a hero. I, of course, did nothing but watch.'

Karla folded her paws in a thoughtful way. Her soft voice beckoned Rana nearer.

'Nothing but watch? But isn't *watching* important?'

Rana paused. It seemed an odd question. 'Well, we all watch,' she said. 'We have to, all the time, to stay safe.'

'But we all watch differently,' Karla replied. 'In the fight with the bear, what did you see?'

Rana was lying so low on the ground, she had almost sunk into it. 'Oh, a great victory for the pack,' she said, in a hollow voice. Then she put on a stronger, boastful drawl. 'The mangy beast didn't stand a chance. It ran away like a stung squirrel!'

Karla tilted her head, impressed. 'That was rather a good impression of Gripper,' she said. 'Now, tell me what you really saw. Tell me about the ferocious grizzly.'

Rana peeped up. 'Well, he *was* ferocious, but—' There was a long pause. Memories rushed through Rana's mind.

'It's the "but" I want to hear.'

Now, Rana spoke as if to herself. 'He was an old bear. Very old—with only one good eye. His hide was hanging loosely over his bones, as if he was wearing his big brother's fur. His face was battered and bashed, as if a herd of elk had been walking across it. In fact, his face looked sad. Sad and sorry at losing the fight. Sad at having to fight at all. That's what I thought. When they all chased him off, I even felt sorry for him.'

'Hmm . . .' Karla rose from her comfy bed of ferns. 'I wasn't there, but I know Old Greyface. And from your details, I'd say that you watched rather well. Come on, let's go back to the party. Show of strength, and all that.'

There was a twinkle in her eyes that Rana liked.

*

When they returned to the party, Rana could feel something was in the air. The mood had changed. Darkmane had placed one of his big forepaws on the skull of the elk. Sunstreak was beside him. Everywolf had formed a circle around them.

'Are we going to tell them?' Sunstreak was asking Darkmane.

'What do you think?' he replied.

The two pack leaders exchanged a long look and then nodded.

'You speak first,' said Sunstreak. 'This elk is your find. These are your woods.'

Darkmane gave a bow of respect to Sunstreak and rose up with both paws on the skull. The broken horns spread out on either side, framing him against the blue twilight and the first stars.

'Friends and family,' he said. 'Kin of fur and blood. I have news for you. This is the day of the wolf!'

A great howl arose from the circled packs.

'Today, together, we drove off a grizzly. We tasted victory against Greyface, the Old Man of the Woods. What is more, Fera guided us to this great elk feast, our best in many a moon.'

Another wild howl erupted.

'Everywhere, our packs run free, not just Starlight and Sundown, but our kin over the ridge and up on the mountain. The whole world is our hunting ground. There is no creature to outrun, outhunt, outfight us. As the old legends say: this land is ours!'

There was more great excitement.

'And now, for some even greater news. For a long time, our pack, the Starlight wolves, have run alongside the Sundown pack, in friendship. Now, the time has come to extend that friendship.' He nodded at Sunstreak to join in.

She stepped forward. 'In recent weeks, we have met the leaders of the five other packs that dwell in Hunter's Reach.'

'These leaders have a noble idea,' said Darkmane. 'To unite all our packs to form one great tribe. All wolves will be one big family, and nothing—not even the great bears—will be able to stand against us.'

'We will have nothing to fear,' said Sunstreak.

'And everything will fear us!' bayed Gripper, from the front of the watching crowd. There was a titanic roar, followed by a long, drawn-out howl. When the excitement had died down, Darkmane spoke again.

'The leaders of the packs will form a council of

Seven Fangs at Howling Rock, by the Mountains of Dawn. There we shall make a Great Den among the caves, where our tiny cubs and our very old can stay safe. Packs will still patrol their old territory, but always have a home to go back to. None will dare attack the Great Den. We will share our strength, our kills and our hardships. In greater numbers, we will be rulers of all we survey!'

Rana ducked out of the way, as Fenn—giddy with excitement—leapt over her. Everywhere, wolves were bounding, capering, howling . . .

But not Karla. Rana could see the old wolf on the edge of the throng, peering around her with a long face. What was she thinking? Rana wanted to be as excited as everywolf else, but—somewhere in her mind, there was a 'but'.

Ayala jumped on Rana, as she had done when Rana was a cub, and gave her an affectionate tumble in the grass. 'Rulers of the forest!' cried Ayala. 'Everywolf safe!' She smiled. 'It's what I dreamed of for you, when you were little.' She watched as Rana scrambled back to her feet. 'It's why you've turned out so soft. I protected you too much.'

Her mother rushed off to join the celebrations.

Rana padded slowly over to the edge of the clearing, where Karla stood.

'All the wolves joining forces,' Rana said, in an awed whisper. 'It sounds like a very wise idea! Did they ask you about it?'

'Of course not,' said Karla. She ducked her head away and moved off into the long grass. 'Come with me.'

CHAPTER 2

It was a far longer journey than Rana had expected. The old she-wolf led her up the long track by the creek, until it crossed a stony way at the foot of one of the long mountain spurs. Here, they sprang up a great fall of boulders, which brought them to a new, higher track. Karla, for all her years, suddenly seemed to possess the energy of a young wolf, swift and untiring.

The slim moon was shining brightly now, rising above low cloud, and the sky was full of stars. As they climbed higher and higher, Rana could still hear the pack whooping below, but growing fainter. A seed of fear began to grow in her. Shouldn't one of the fiercer wolves have come with them? Maybe two? Suppose they met a cougar?

On a rocky ledge, overlooking the tops of the valley pines, Karla stopped and looked back at Rana. She seemed to have read the younger wolf's mind. 'You will be safe on this track,' she said quietly. Rana immediately felt better and trotted along happily.

Karla glanced over her shoulder again. 'It is a bad place,' she added. 'None come here.'

Now *that* wasn't so great. Rana pondered the remark as she ran along, her mind popping with unasked questions. She felt anxious and exhausted when they finally stopped on a high crag, about halfway up the mountain spur.

'Sit,' said Karla. 'Rest.'

Rana noticed that there were no trees, no scrub. In fact, no signs of any life at all. 'Why have we come here?' she asked. 'Why is this a bad place?'

Karla didn't reply. She sat in a comfortable, curled shape and invited Rana to sit before her. The echoing howls of the pack were faint but still comfortingly within earshot. The barren rock caught the moonlight in an unusual way, surrounding them with an eerie radiance.

'You know, my dear, about the Order of Stories, don't you?'

'Yes,' said Rana, brightly. 'The littlest cubs get the First Stories, like *The Big Tasty Bison*. Then when they get older, they get the Warning Stories, like *Goldenfur and the Three Grizzlies*. Ouch—harsh ending on *that*.'

Karla nodded. 'There are also tales that many wolves are never told. They are Forbidden Stories.'

Rana was silent. Her heart was beating fast. Was she going to hear a Forbidden Story?

Karla had a faraway look in her eyes, as she stared over the treetops, away to the stars. 'You are my best listener. You will be a storyteller one day.'

A tingle of excitement ran up Rana's spine. She would be a storyteller? The idea filled her with a warm glow. Could it be true? Or was Karla just being kind?

'Fenn tells much better stories than me,' Rana said.

'Taller stories, perhaps,' said Karla. 'But not truer. You have the power to tell things as they truly are,' she added. 'And that is rare.'

The night became quiet. The pack had ceased

howling. Rana no longer felt anxious or tired, but full of expectation. She was the best listener? Then she would show Karla how well she could listen.

'You asked me about joining the packs together,' said Karla. 'I know all about this plan, although I was not consulted.'

'How did you know?'

'A raven told me,' Karla replied.

Rana was wide-eyed. 'You talk to ravens?'

'Yes—and so could you. All creatures have the same tongue, one just needs the ears to hear. It is only through years of prejudice and mistrust that most wolves now only talk among themselves.'

Rana's eyes lit up. Karla always had something to say that opened up a way to a more exciting world. She nodded, eager to hear more.

'There was a time in the past when the wolves were united. A Far-off Time before the great pine was split and before Last Rock was an island.'

Rana felt a shiver. She was fascinated by the Far-off Times.

'In those days, wolves reigned supreme over all the forest. Their leader was Frost, bravest of the brave. She was so ferocious that her pack, the Sunrise, ruled all others, from the mountains to the sea. They made a Great Den in the heart of the Eternal Forest. Prey was plentiful and the pack was blessed with many cubs. It was a golden time for wolves. All other creatures feared them, even the bears.

'With no worries of the usual kind, like hunger and competition, their world became a paradise, and Frost was revered as a god—some even saying she was Fera, the First Wolf, reborn in mortal shape.

'Stories of this great pack spread far and wide. And the fame and glory of the pack eventually reached envious ears.

'Then one night, many shooting stars appeared. The wolves howled with delight at the spectacle. But these stars did not flash across the sky and fade like shooting stars usually did. They grew brighter, steadier—and came nearer.

'All at once, the Eternal Forest was aflame. The stars had landed. They were not stars at all, but dragons—creatures bigger than bears, with bat-like wings and gleaming eyes. Their hides were scaly and tough, their talons were sharp. And they could breathe fire.

'Frost herself was among the first to die, as the dragons torched the Sunrise den and all within. It had been too grand—too easy to find. Frost's people sought to flee to all corners of the forest, but their ways were too well-made, too well-trodden, too clear. They were easily found by the dragons, who hunted the fleeing wolves and slew them with ease.

'When the dragons believed that the last wolf was dead, they burned the forest to the ground, then rose on their dark wings, disappearing back into the night. A rival kingdom was destroyed. A greater glory than their own was now ashes. They were content.

'Only one small group of survivors limped from the smoking wreck of their old paradise. They learned to live without glory and plenty, and without a Great Den. Instead, they had hunger, and hiding, and wandering. And so, a new era began . . . at Hunter's Reach.'

The night fell silent. Rana gazed ahead, spellbound. She no longer saw Karla, but the Far-off Time and all its perils and wonders.

'It's just a story, isn't it?' she asked at last.

Karla peered out into the night. 'It is a Forbidden Story,' she said. 'One that wolves are not supposed to tell, except in times of great need. It brings nightmares, uncertainty, fear.'

'So, it's a scary story that some wolves don't like to hear,' Rana said, then added, 'but it *is* just a story, isn't it?'

'For now,' said the old she-wolf. 'But there is no such thing as *just a story*.' She turned away. 'Come!'

Rana found herself following Karla once more, up the stony path. They reached a dark crack in the side of the mountain, wide enough for several bears to enter all at once. Karla sniffed carefully, then padded inside. Rana was reluctant to follow but summoned just enough courage to go on.

'Is this a bad place too?' asked Rana.

Karla nodded. 'There is a tomb cave beyond here, full of the bones of wolves long dead. It is a dread place where nowolf goes. But here, the outer cave has a special secret. Keep close!'

Rana followed Karla along a ledge up to a bare rock face. In fact, on closer inspection it wasn't bare at all, but covered in deep, twisting marks.

As Rana's eyes grew more accustomed to the darkness, she realised something. The marks formed a great spiral.

Rana frowned. 'What can make a cut like this in rock?' she asked.

'It isn't a cut,' said Karla. 'Look, it's smooth, like it's been melted.'

Rana's fur stood on end, but her big eyes peered up. 'What can melt rock? Maybe . . . lightning?'

Karla turned away. 'Lightning has not been known to draw circles.'

Together they stood in the gloom, the old storyteller and the yearling, gripped by the enigma of the vast, twisting shape.

'The only thing I can think of that could make these marks,' said Karla, 'is dragon fire.'

CHAPTER 3

Rana forgot all about the Forbidden Story in the excitement of the following days. The prospect of the seven packs joining forces was all anyone could talk about.

On the day of the next full moon, as twilight began to fall, Rana's ears pricked up at an argument.

'You don't have to go!' It was Karla, talking to Darkmane.

'Yes, we do.'

'It's a mistake,' the old storyteller said. 'The old tales say—'

'Forget the old tales!' snapped Darkmane. 'This is about real life, here and now. The Starlight pack needs allies. The cave lions have been seen on our borders. They are fierce foes who will kill to take territory they want. With food scarce, we need to be united and strong. Stories don't feed hungry bellies.'

'Look on the bright side,' said her mother, who had joined the conversation. 'There'll be so many more wolves to tell your stories to!'

Karla humphed at this.

Darkmane addressed the pack who had gathered around in curiosity. 'I will leave now, accompanied by Gripper and Lightfoot. We proceed to Howling Rock, the sacred place of the wolves. If the seven packs agree to unite, we shall howl from its peak. Listen out, when the moon is high.'

The chosen three loped off into the night. Ayala was left in charge of Starlight. The pack was a little more excitable in Darkmane's absence, so Rana helped divert the cubs by telling them the story of *The Deer Who Came to Tea*.

As twilight deepened, her mother gathered the remaining pack together.

'This is an important night for wolves,' Ayala said. 'I am taking us up to Broken Ridge. You can see Howling Rock from there. If the packs do agree to unite, it will be the perfect place to hear the great howl echo over the valley.'

'Come on, Rana,' said Fenn. 'All the yearlings are racing to get there first!'

Rana saw Fenn rush off after Ela and Riki. After a moment's hesitation, she joined in the race. Arriving at the top, Rana felt a sense of awe.

The full moon was just peeping over the Mountains of the Dawn. The great forest stretched out below, bathed in cold light. Beyond the rows of pines, a dark spire of stone was silhouetted against the stars: Howling Rock. The four young wolves contemplated the view—and the future.

'Do you want the packs to unite, Rana?' asked Fenn. 'Imagine running alongside Stalker Pack, with their leader, Sly! What a brute! He is supposed to be the fiercest wolf ever. And the youngest pack leader ever! I'd love to see him in action. What about you?'

'Well,' said Rana. 'I'd like to meet the storytellers from the other packs. Maybe they know wonderful old tales that—'

'Yawn, yawn, yawn!' butted in Ela. 'Storytelling is just for cubs. Don't you agree, Riki?' She looked at her crony for his usual support. 'We could be running the hunt with top wolves every day. Plotting ambushes instead of catching fleas off riff-raff.' She glanced at Fenn and Rana.

Riki snickered.

The older wolves began to arrive. Silence fell as the moon rose higher. It had never looked so large. Its pale yellow face was softened by a thin haze.

'Soon we'll know.' Rana sighed. There was a moment of anti-climax when a nightjar sent out its lonely song, prompting Fenn to wail along briefly, then stop in embarrassment.

'Hey, I knew that wasn't the great howl!' Fenn said.

'Shush,' said Rana. 'You are kind of ruining the moment.'

Silence fell again. Rana noticed that the night had deepened, bringing the stars out more clearly in the sky. Then it began, an eerie, far-off sound, rising and falling; the familiar cry of Darkmane himself. Immediately other wolves joined in, some harsher, more shrill and higher-pitched. Others low, and so mournful it made your fur stand on end. Echoing among the valleys and ravines, the howling told the tale of a historic moment. The wolves had united.

Ayala led the Starlight pack in a great howl in reply.

It felt like one of the biggest moments of Rana's life.

Just then, as she gazed over at Howling Rock, she spotted something in the sky. There, among the stars, a brighter light was moving—fast. Glowing red, it left a faint trail.

'A shooting star!' said Fenn.

'A lucky omen,' said Ayala.

Rana felt a tingle in her bones. Right now, a shooting star was not top of the list of things she wanted to see.

'It's coming this way!' yelped Fenn.

The star should have faded by now, but it was growing brighter. It really was coming closer. The wolves began to howl with excitement. Rana did not feel the same way. She looked around for Karla, who was nowhere to be seen. Rana found herself trembling with anxiety. Her ears were flat against her head.

'Look at Rana, she's terrified!' said Ela.

'Poor Rana, it's only a twinkly little star,' said Riki in a babyish voice.

'There!' Ayala said.

The star had fallen to earth in the forest—somewhere near the Rushing Waters.

'Fell in the river, I think,' said Fenn, gazing after it.

'Funny, for a moment it gave me a creepy feeling—' He frowned, then turned away. 'Oh, forget about it. Come on, the packs have teamed up! Soon I'll be best friends with Sly.'

The wolves whooped and headed off down the ridge, none of them noticing that Rana was still standing, staring into the gloom. She had seen Karla. The older wolf was racing away from the pack, in the direction of where the star had fallen.

She is worried, thought Rana. *She has to see for herself.* The other wolves had already disappeared, over the hill. Karla, who meant the world to Rana, was charging into danger and uncertainty.

Suddenly, something inside Rana cracked. She would not be the scared one, the teased one, the wolf who stayed behind where it was safe. She was a storyteller too, like Karla, and she had to witness things. She had to be with her friend. Unseen by the rest of her pack, Rana vanished into the night.

It took all Rana's speed and stamina to keep Karla in sight. At the bottom of the first gorge, she saw the old wolf vanishing over the ridge ahead. When she topped that ridge, panting for breath, she saw Karla's tail disappearing under the eaves of the pine forest. For a while, Rana relied on scent alone to track Karla along the overgrown path that led down to Bear River. As she emerged from the tangle of the trees, she saw the storyteller ahead, moving more slowly now, picking a way through marshy ground.

Rana's heart was pounding. She had never been so far from the rest of her pack, but the sight of Karla ahead kept her brave. She was gaining on her quarry now, as the old she-wolf kept stopping to sniff the air.

As they approached the tall stand of pines where Bear River turned into the rocky rapids of the Rushing Waters, Rana was relieved to see no sign of a forest fire, although there was a vague trace of smoke drifting among the tops of the trees.

Then Rana broke through a patch of dark scrub and almost bumped into Karla, who had come to a dead stop just ahead. She was gazing up at an unusual sight.

From here on, the pine forest was devastated. Splintered tree stumps stood out against the starry sky, forming a strangely perfect line. Smashed debris was scattered on all signs, looking charred and giving off wisps of smoke. Something had hit this part of the forest at incredible speed, and cut through solid trees as if they were straw.

'Rana!' The old wolf had turned and was looking back at her with dark eyes. 'What are you doing here?'

Rana's heart sank at her friend's fierce tone, and she crept apologetically, ears flattened, looking a little away from Karla.

'I-I couldn't let you go alone!'

'Great,' snapped Karla. 'Now I have two things to worry about. The shooting star and you.'

Rana's determination came back in a rush and she ran to her friend's side.

'I'm here to help,' she said, and remembering a phrase from one of Karla's own stories, said, 'Nowolf should ever be alone.'

Karla sighed and let her mouth hang open in a kind of crooked smile.

'Well, if you are going to quote my own work at me . . .'

Rana smiled too. The two wolves padded closer to the strange, broken section of forest.

'It has come down near here,' Karla said softly, pointing with her snout at the smashed pines. 'If we keep going, following the line of stumps, we should find it . . . whatever it is.'

They trotted into the edge of the wood, springing over the broken branches, twigs and debris that blanketed the ground.

'Look!'

The line of wrecked trees ended in a scene of utter ruin. Shattered trunks were strewn upon the ground, laid out like flowers flattened by spring snow. In the middle, a dark crater yawned. Smoke was rising from it.

'Have you ever seen a fallen star before?' asked Rana.

Karla shook her head. 'Usually, they just pass overhead,' she said. 'There is a story from the Snowfoot pack of a wolf finding a star-stone inside the ice at the top of a mountain. A beautiful thing! The whole pack came to gaze at it. I hope that's all we find here. Now, let me—'

But Karla was interrupted. They both stopped in their tracks, as some way ahead a wolf, pale in the light of the full moon, came racing into view.

'Lightfoot!' said Rana, whose young eyes were the sharpest.

Karla gestured with her head for Rana to stay back.

'Of course! The wolves at Howling Rock will have sent runners out to check the site too.'

Rana felt a sense of relief as several other wolves arrived on the heels of Lightfoot. None of them spotted the two friends.

'There's Sly!' said Karla, pointing with her snout at a burly, dark wolf with a bushy tail and one crooked ear. 'He's the chief of Stalker pack.'

Rana crept nearer for a better view.

'That's good, isn't it?'

'I don't know,' Karla whispered. 'Wolves that run fastest don't always have the quickest minds.' Unseen, they listened to the arriving wolves.

'Stand back,' panted Sly, who seemed to have had trouble keeping up with the others. 'I'm the only chief here and I'll take over.'

'You're not my chief,' said Lightfoot. 'And I got here first. I'm going to take a look.'

Lightfoot moved towards the smoke that was drifting up from the crater.

'You'll do as I say!' growled Sly.

'Huh!' said Lightfoot. 'Why should you get all the glory?'

Rana's fur stood on end as she crept forward. She

and Karla were on a ridge of slightly higher ground looking down on the scene. Lightfoot and Sly were vanishing into the smoke. All was quiet, apart from the distant thunder of the Rushing Waters.

A sudden yelp from Sly broke the silence. There was a whine from Lightfoot. The two wolves came dashing out of the smoke.

'There's something in there!' gasped Lightfoot.

Had Rana imagined it, or was a shadow moving in the smoke?

'They do not know the danger,' cried Karla, backing away.

Rana stared into the murk, transfixed. She remained on the ridge, as the smoky vapours rose and twisted in the air, and she lost lost sight of Karla.

'Rana, where are you?' yelped Karla.

Below, Lightfoot and Sly were circling the crater in a kind of panic. Rana could not help but watch. The greatest story of her lifetime was unfolding below her, right now. How could she look away?

The shape in the smoke was clearer now, bigger than a grizzly, but spiky, twisted, broken. It was shambling around in an awkward way, as if it could barely stand up.

'Rana, be careful!' shouted Karla.

Through the murk, Rana saw red flame crackle in a pair of jagged jaws. Suddenly, the world was full of blinding light—and she knew no more.

CHAPTER 4

Rana was in a meadow, following a butterfly. It was a pretty one, but unusual—dark blue with white spiral markings on its wings. She felt that this meant something, but couldn't remember what.

'Are you hunting me?' the butterfly asked.

'No, I'm not hunting you,' said Rana, with a smile. 'I was looking for something. A fallen star, I think.'

'A fallen star?' said the butterfly.

Rana frowned. 'Yes, but it isn't really a star. It's a creature, or something.' Rana tried hard to remember.

The butterfly settled on a blade of grass, letting its wings feel the sun. 'If it fell from the sky, it must be hurt. It will need your help.'

Rana racked her brains. 'It's a magical creature,' she said at last. 'Out of a story. It could be dangerous. How could *I* help it?'

'If it's something out of a story, maybe another story will show you the way,' said the butterfly.

Rana pondered this. She needed to ask Karla for more stories. But where was Karla? In fact, where was everywolf? Why was she alone in this big meadow with a talking butterfly?

As she questioned her surroundings, she began to awaken. Light was peeping from somewhere and tickling her eyelids.

'Rana?'

She recognised that voice. She began to notice the fragrance of sweet herbs. She was lying on a bed of dry grasses in a cave of some kind.

'What happened?'

'Where do I begin?' Karla sighed.

Rana tried to look around, but it sent a burning pain through her neck.

'Don't move,' Karla said gently.

'Where am I?'

'We're in one of the dens at Howling Rock. This is where they brought us after you were hurt.'

Rana tried to remember what had happened, but her mind did not want to go there. Her head was a throbbing muddle of images.

'The thing,' she said. 'The thing in the crater!'

'Don't worry about it now,' said Karla. 'Try to rest.'

Rana could feel a tongue licking and fussing about her mane. Before she knew it, she was asleep again.

It was dark when Rana next awoke. Someone had left her a juicy deer bone to gnaw. She could smell the scent of her mother, so she guessed Ayala had been to see her. Karla was by her side, and soon noticed that she had stirred.

'How do you feel, little one?'

'Not too bad,' said Rana, her voice a small, dry croak. 'How badly was I hurt?'

'You'll live.' Karla smiled. 'No bones broken—but your mane will probably never be the same again.'

Rana brought a hind paw up to her neck and felt only a scraggy stubble.

'You had an encounter with a star-creature,' Karla said. 'Fire blasted out of the crater, over the heads of the other wolves. You were still up on the ridge and caught the very edge of it. Let's call it a lucky escape.'

'When you say a star-creature . . . ?'

'I think I might have another name for it,' said Karla. 'But it's hard to say for certain. We have been shut out.'

'What do you mean?'

'After you were hurt, the creature collapsed. Many more wolves arrived from Howling Rock. The creature was dragged away.'

'But—is everything alright? Are we safe?'

Karla looked away. 'I don't know,' she said. 'The chief wolves have formed a council. They are keeping their discovery secret, for now. Only they know what's going on.'

'Can we go and find out?' asked Rana, rising shakily to her feet.

'No,' said Karla, choosing that moment to flop down in a huff. 'For now, I've been told to stay here and look after you. Oh, and not to talk to anywolf.'

Familiar pawsteps echoed through the den shortly after, and Darkmane appeared.

'Where have you been?' snapped Karla.

'Nice to see you too,' said Darkmane. He gave Rana an affectionate nuzzle and looked her over.

Karla confronted him. 'Come on, Chief! Spill it. What was going on at the site of the shooting star? Why did you let Sly take over?'

Darkmane scowled and sat down; he had an air of weariness, yet infinite patience. He spoke slowly.

'Sly hasn't taken over. When we saw the shooting star land, every chief chose their fastest runner to get to the site as quickly as possible. It was a very sensible approach. Except Sly decided to choose himself. He's like that. I followed later, but you were busy looking after Rana. Why you were there in the first place—'

'Because we care about what happens to this pack!' Karla exploded. 'The star is a source of grave danger. What has happened to the creature, by the way?'

'I can't talk about it. Council business is very secret, at the moment.'

'But we know all about your secret, we were there! Where is the creature? Is it alive? What are you all playing at?'

'We are not "playing" at anything. It is a most serious matter,' Darkmane said. 'You two are going to be summoned shortly.'

'Summoned?' scoffed Karla. 'I like that! You have only united the packs for one day and you are already giving yourselves airs. The council! Secrets! Summoning us!'

'Oh, give me a break, Karla!' groaned Darkmane. 'It's been a long day.'

Rana couldn't help but smile. It was good to hear her father bickering with Karla, as usual. It made life seem more normal again.

'*I* don't mind being summoned, Dad,' Rana said. 'After that, can I go home?'

Darkmane gave her a curious look. 'You don't seem to understand. This is Howling Rock. This is our home now. Everything has changed.' He looked at Karla. 'And we all have to learn to like it.'

CHAPTER 5

Just as dawn was breaking, Darkmane and Sunstreak came to fetch them.

'Well, we are very privileged,' said Karla. 'All this attention from pack chiefs!'

'There is only one pack now—the Great Pack,' said Sunstreak. 'Before you meet the others, we have to take you somewhere very special.'

She led the way. Howling Rock was riddled with cracks and honeycombed with caves of all sizes. It echoed with the movement of the many wolves already there, the leaders, their lieutenants and some runners.

On the ground floor, just above the level of the

dens, Sunstreak ducked into a low passage. It was a little chilly here, but a fresh scent filled the air. As they entered, a glimmer of light greeted their eyes. There was a pool of water at the far side, fed by some unseen, underground stream. The pool reflected the pale light from a distant shaft above. Rana noticed that Karla was gazing up at the wall as if spellbound. What was she looking at?

Peering closely, Rana noticed there were colours in the rock, glittering threads of different stones woven through each other. There was a great deal of red stone among the grey. Rana began to see that the red stone formed the head of a great she-wolf. With open jaws, the shape seemed frozen in time, baying at an eternal night sky. Little specks of glittering minerals formed tiny stars around the wolf's head.

'You are in the Sacred Place of Fera,' said Sunstreak. 'Here you will swear to be loyal to the Great Pack forever.'

Rana kept staring up at the image of the First Wolf. It was more beautiful than anything she had ever seen.

Darkmane eyed Karla. 'Are you going to swear, old friend? I know that you were not happy with the idea of all the packs uniting.'

Karla bowed her head. 'It is childish to expect to be happy all the time,' she said. 'You have to run with the pack, as all wolves know. I swear.'

Rana was relieved. She was very happy to declare her loyalty in that beautiful place. In fact, as she swore her loyalty, she felt big inside, as if she were going to burst.

On the same ground level was the entrance to a much larger space. Rana peered past the guard wolf to see a high ceiling disappearing into dark shadows and echoes.

'You are about to enter the Chamber of the Seven Fangs,' Darkmane said softly. 'This is where I meet in council with the other pack leaders. Do you remember their names?'

Rana rolled her eyes. All the Starlight pack wolves learned this as cubs. She recited, 'Sly from Stalker pack, Silver from Snowfoot, Sunstreak from Sunrise,' she paused as Sunstreak nodded her acknowledgment, then continued, 'Chiggers from Cowbird pack, Haze from Horizon, and Hunter from Lightning.'

'Very good,' said Darkmane. 'Now, we had better not keep them waiting.'

Inside the chamber, five wolves sat on tall rocks that gave them an imposing air. Darkmane and Sunstreak sprang into position to complete the Seven Fangs.

In the centre sat one very old, grey wolf. He had a narrow face that looked as if it had been worn sharp by the winter winds of the mountains he came from. His whiskers were white, and his fur was mottled and patchy.

'Is this your Rana?' the old wolf asked in a creaky voice. Darkmane grunted in affirmative. The old wolf beckoned with a gnarled claw.

'Let us see you!'

Rana crept forward, feeling the weight of all the important eyes on her. A couple of the chiefs muttered as they saw what remained of her mane.

'My name is Silver,' croaked the old wolf. 'The uniting of the packs was my idea. I have great hopes and dreams for us all.'

'We have sworn loyalty to the Great Pack.' Karla stepped forward. 'Now, kindly tell us what in Fera's name is going on!'

There was a murmur among the pack leaders.

'An extraordinary event marked the night of our unity,' said Silver. 'A moment of destiny. And you two were present. I am most interested in matters of destiny. How did you happen to be there?'

'We are storytellers,' said Karla. 'Shooting stars can bring good luck or bad. When this one landed close to us, it was our duty to witness it.'

Silver looked slowly at his fellow chiefs.

'I have never heard of a shooting star bringing bad luck,' he said at last. 'I believe we have been blessed.'

'Not all tales and superstitions are known to all wolves,' said Karla.

Silver appeared to ignore this. He lowered his grey head and spoke softly.

'A star-creature has fallen in our midst. You—' he glanced at Rana, 'have had an encounter with it. I believe your injury was an accident, from a stranger much confused and hurt.'

'It was one heck of an accident,' said Karla. A few feet lower and it would have barbecued most of the wolves there.'

'But it did not,' Silver said meaningfully. 'Destiny was kind.'

A few other wolves murmured in agreement.

'We brought the creature back to Howling Rock,' said Sly, the burly young wolf Rana recognised from the night before. 'And a lot of wolves it took to move it! We have it trapped in the most secure cave here.'

'Our first impulse was to keep this discovery as secret as possible,' Silver said. 'A star-creature, if befriended, could serve us well. It must also be . . . protected.'

'But the creature has not stirred,' said Haze, an older female. 'In fact, it appears to be dying. After some debate, it occurred to us that the ancient lore of our storytellers might help us understand it, even heal it.'

At a nod from Silver, the seven wolves sprang down from their rocks.

'Come and see!'

Rana found herself being led higher up the network of caverns, until she was in a chamber right at the top of Howling Rock's great spire. A jagged crack in one wall let in the pale morning light.

A row of stalactites, shiny teeth of rock, hung

along the far wall of the chamber. They reached down to a ledge beneath, forming a natural cage of stone. This had been deliberately blocked at one end by several heavy boulders. Inside, lay a dark shape—a little larger than a grizzly bear, but longer and more sinuous.

At first, Rana mistook it for a strange, twisted rock. But then she saw the rock move. It was breathing. Gradually, her eyes got used to the gloom and she made out a head, its face cast in a look of pain. Awkwardly folded limbs shifted among the shadows. Jutting from one side was a crooked shape, like a bat wing but impossibly large. It looked twisted and broken.

Without thinking, Rana spoke the word she'd hoped never to speak, and as she did, everywolf turned to look at her.

'A dragon!'

In the shadows of its prison, the injured creature suddenly stirred. It raised a saurian head on a smooth, scaly neck and opened one sleepy eye.

Rana had never seen such an eye, a kaleidoscope of greens and blues—from aqua to emerald, through to violet and midnight blue.

And the eye was staring at her.

'How do you know what I am?' the dragon asked in a dry whisper.

Then the head slumped down again, in sleep.

CHAPTER 6

The pack leaders surrounded Rana. They had moved from the top cave, back down to the Chamber of the Seven Fangs. Rana's legs felt shaky as all those sharp eyes stared at her. She crouched as low as she could with her tail tucked under. Only the thought of Karla beside her prevented her from running away.

'How *do* you know what that thing is?' asked Sly, his tone suspicious.

Rana could not find her tongue. She gave a whimper and looked at Karla.

'She knows because I told her,' said Karla. 'Leave her alone!'

'What is a . . . dur-a-gon?' Silver asked slowly. The old wolf had a spellbound look as he stared from Rana to Karla and back again.

'They are in the old stories,' said Karla. 'It is a devil. Kill it now.'

At this, a murmur went through the council, and they all exchanged looks.

'Kill it? Why?' asked Darkmane.

'Ancient lore warns that dragons are tyrants who use powerful magic to bring destruction on all other realms,' said Karla. 'Listen well, and I will share with you a Forbidden Story. Then you will understand my mistrust.'

A hush fell over the chamber as the old storyteller told the Seven Fangs the tale Rana had heard just days earlier. Even the high stone walls seemed to listen as she described how, in Far-off Times, the great realm of the legendary chief Frost was discovered and then destroyed by dragons.

'It is an evil creature that can bring only doom to our kind,' Karla summarised. 'Where there is one, more will follow—if they get the chance. Destroy your dragon now, before it escapes to lead dragonkind in war against us once again. Unless we heed Frost's

Forbidden Story, Hunter's Reach will burn to ashes and the Great Pack will be slaughtered.'

'An ominous tale indeed,' said Sunstreak. 'Thank you, Karla. We must consider this wisdom carefully.'

Rana and Karla waited outside the chamber as the Seven Fangs debated. Finally, Darkmane called them back.

'A dragon can be dangerous,' said Silver. 'But then, so can a storm. Yet storms sometimes bring much-needed rain, or blow down great trees—leaving a perfect den under the upturned roots. What if this dragon is destined to return our realm to the paradise it was in the Far-off Time of Frost?'

'This dur-a-gon has a great magic,' said Sly. 'The power of fire. If we can keep it alive and befriend it, imagine what an ally it would be!'

'Perhaps it has other magical powers too. We must find out,' Haze added.

Karla scowled. 'Greed for power will only bring evil upon us all,' she said.

'There are other reasons,' said Sunstreak. 'Imagine if you were hurt, in a strange land. You would not wish to be slain because of old superstitions and cub-stories!'

Despite herself, Rana liked Sunstreak's words, and her heart grew hopeful. For what, she did not know. But wasn't it always better to be kind?

'Surely nothing is evil, of itself,' said Darkmane. 'A claw may be used to kill or to give a helping paw. What will Fera expect of us?'

'To kill dragons!' snapped Karla. Her words hung in the air, while the council huddled for further debate. At last, Darkmane spoke to Rana and Karla once more.

'We will watch the dragon further before making a decision,' he announced. 'If it makes fire and troubles us, we may well do as Karla says. But if it is too sick to do so, and attempts no harm, there is hope it can be befriended. Rana is wounded, so until she is healed she is to stay at Howling Rock with you, Karla, to care for her.'

Karla nodded her assent, but her stiff tail showed her disapproval.

'If you are hungry, ask a guard to send a runner for anything you like. But don't go anywhere near that thing again until we tell you.'

'This is the life,' said Karla, chewing on the haunch

of a deer. The pair were sitting in a little cave near the Chamber of the Seven Fangs. 'I could get used to being waited on.'

Rana had just finished the leg of a wild turkey. 'What, living in this place?' she asked. 'It's too cold and stony! I'd rather be outside in the sunshine.'

'Well, you'll never have to be cold again,' said Karla. 'If we keep that dragon alive, we'll have a constant source of cosy fire to warm our paws with.'

Rana pulled a face. 'You don't mean that. Anyway, I don't think it's going to be that simple!'

'Neither do I,' said Karla. 'But I don't think for a moment that greedy wolves like Sly and Silver will kill it, whatever I say. They've heard of its magical fire. Sly has even seen it.'

'So have I,' said Rana. 'Sort of!'

'Myself also,' said Karla. 'And thank Fera we survived. But the Seven Fangs are much intrigued by the fire. I've seen the magic-lust in their eyes. It might even be in yours,' she added. 'Show me your eyes.'

Rana laughed and covered her eyes with her paws. 'Shan't,' she joked.

'See? You're already getting rebellious,' said Karla.

'It's the dragon effect.' But her eyes twinkled.

The older wolf seemed less fearsome now, than the angry Karla who had wanted the dragon dead. Rana ventured a question.

'Do you really think it is evil? Must it die?'

'A wounded dragon is not like old Greyface, a solitary creature who troubles us little. It is like a cave lion, with a pride of powerful friends whose desire to rule others knows no end. If this creature survives to speak one word of our prosperous realm to any other dragon, then our haven will be no more.'

Karla seemed sad now, not angry. In a way, it made Rana feel worse, like she was trapped in a story that had no happy ending to tell.

'Even if the dragon is not altogether evil,' Karla continued, quietly but firmly, 'it will bring evil upon us. The danger of keeping it alive is too great.'

Rana scratched an ear but stayed silent. She still wasn't sure that killing was the answer. Finally, she spoke.

'But would you really . . . ?'

'Kill it?' Karla sighed. 'I would not wish to harm any helpless creature, except to spare it pain and suffering. The dragon is sorely wounded—unable to fly and too weak to hunt. A swift death would end its misery, and protect the pack. Who knows, perhaps that is what Fera will bring it.'

The old wolf nodded towards the chamber. 'It is only greed that is making Silver and the others want to look after it. You wait and see. The dragon will bring out the worst in them. Oh dear, my little one, whatever are we going to do?'

The next morning, they were summoned to the chamber again. Dawn was starting to break, and a pale light peeped through the many cracks and splits in the ancient stone. Here, Darkmane and another wolf awaited them.

'You storytellers are going to be our spokeswolves to the dragon,' said Darkmane. 'We have decided the dragon is a creature from the Far-off Times, which only storytellers really understand. You will get to know him, find out what powers he has, and convince him to use them to help the pack. We have summoned Old Lupey, the Cowbird pack storyteller, to help you. The Seven Fangs will tell you what to say and so on.'

'That's good, isn't it?' said Rana, looking up at

Karla. 'For once, they really need wolves like us.'

'It's a new one for me,' said Lupey, a thin old wolf with long whiskers. 'Normally, storytellers don't get such respect! Not in my pack, anyway.'

'Respect!' snorted Karla. 'Don't you see? They're all afraid of his fire. Tales of such monsters always have a high body count—usually of roasted wolves. That's why the Seven Fangs are happy to put us in the front line. One sneeze and—poof! They're not stupid.'

'Thanks, Karla.' Rana sighed. 'I feel so much better!'

Lupey chuckled. 'Things don't always turn out as bad as you think,' he said. 'Stand behind me and hope for the best.'

The dragon's cave was filled with a cold grey light. The other pack leaders prowled it nervously. The stone cage took up less than a quarter of the space, but the dragon's presence seemed to fill the room. Rana could see the scaly creature more clearly now. Standing, it would probably be over three times taller than she was, but collapsed on the ground, it looked broken, almost lifeless. Pity filled her heart. The wolves approached gingerly.

'The beast is on the brink of death,' whispered

Karla. 'Kill it now, it will be a mercy!'

'Shush, don't make it mad,' quavered Lupey.

Sly raised a paw and poked the dragon in the side.

'Wake up,' he growled. 'Wake up, dur-a-gon!'

The wolves all jumped as the creature shifted one of its wings. Slowly, it opened both eyes.

'We have decided to spare you,' said Silver. 'If you help us with your magic fire, we will be kind masters. If you try to trick us in any way, you will be wolf-food.'

'You are most kind,' croaked the dragon, feebly.

'These wolves will be your carers,' said Silver. 'They know old and strange things that might be of help to you.'

The dragon raised its head slowly to look at Rana and the older storytellers. It flinched at Karla's expression. 'This grey *skurrimurker* wants to kill me. I can't talk to her.'

Lupey yelped and skittered back as the dragon turned its gaze on him. 'And this scatty one here is too frightened to look at me.'

The dragon collapsed down, looking exhausted and dispirited.

'You will have to talk to somewolf,' growled Silver.

The creature opened one brilliant eye and turned its gaze on Rana.

'I'll talk to *her*,' it said. 'The young *fliffer-hoffer*.'

Karla sprang forward. 'I am not leaving Rana alone with that thing!' she snarled. 'He could eat her in one gulp!'

The dragon gave a weary smile. 'I am not going to eat you,' he said to Rana. 'I am trapped here, and these grumpy old *mubbimurkers* would kill me if I tried. Also, wolf is tough and stringy to eat. I much prefer fish.'

Rana looked at the creature curiously. It seemed to her that it had almost been trying to make a joke. But glancing around, she couldn't see anywolf smiling.

'What do you say?' asked Darkmane. 'Will you do it, Rana?'

Rana looked up into her father's big solemn eyes. Here, in front of the other chiefs, Darkmane had spoken to his daughter like she was an adult of the pack, not an awkward yearling he needed to protect. Rana was almost too astonished to speak.

'Don't!' shouted Karla.

Rana peered back at the helpless dragon, sprawled before them. For a moment, she was reminded of old

Greyface, surrounded by wolves, fearing for his life. A pang of pity for those without a pack of their own touched her heart.

Her father's words stirred another emotion. She was not used to being relied on. Suddenly, she saw a chance to be a new Rana, a brave one that pack leaders actually needed. That would show Ela and Riki, and everywolf who joked about her all the time.

She gave a tiny nod of her head. Karla had to be practically dragged out by the other wolves. The dragon had slumped back to sleep. Rana was left behind in the darkness.

CHAPTER 7

How long had he been here?

The dragon had lost all sense of time. Nearby, he saw the young wolf, the *fliffer-hoffer*, sleeping. A small reminder of the big pack that encircled him.

He felt cramped and uncomfortable in the stone cage that held him. Through bleary eyes, he peered at the stalactites that pointed down from the roof like great knobbly fangs. He was captured alright. Prisoner of a bunch of smelly furballs. How had he, Lyricon, come to this?

He felt something tiny scurry over his tail and he swished it instinctively—immediately banging it against the rocks behind him.

So, there were mice here as well as wolves. Nice.

Slowly rising to a cautious crouch, he found there was just enough room to turn around in the cage. He felt a sharp pang as he tried to move his left wing. That was the broken one. And there was no-one for at least a thousand leagues who knew how to fix it. Would it repair naturally, with a little magical help? He would have to move it as little as possible.

More worrying, if anything, was the sickness he could feel in his every limb. He had multiple cuts and grazes from the crashlanding. Infection could have got in a number of ways. Perhaps from whatever weird mosquitoes they had in this strange land.

How had he ended up crashlanding here, anyway? Had a spell gone wrong? Had he been struck by lightning on one of his more adventurous flights? He began to search his memory for possible clues, but his mind was too muddled. Something would come to him.

Twisting around at the cost of various complaints from his muscles and damaged hide, he looked around the cave with dismay. Dark, dingy, about as big as one of the smaller storerooms back home. The roof was low; even if he got out of this cage, he would have to stoop, standing upright.

Sunlight, he needed sunlight on his wings to restore his magical energies. But he could see that his cage was on the other side of the cave from the cracks in the wall that let in the light.

'Karla is right . . . kill it now . . .'

Sound travelled easily in the warren of tunnels that made up this place they called Howling Rock. And dragons had sharp ears. His captors did not know he could often hear them discussing him. Or maybe they just didn't care.

'He may be as big as three wolves put together,' one voice below was saying. 'But one bite in the neck would do it. His skin looks softer there.'

It chilled his blood. His thoughts raced, filling him with despair.

After a while, the wolf voices went silent. He heard snuffling and snoring from down below. So, they all slept in the midday heat. Knowing those *mubbimurkers* were resting helped him to calm down. They had not killed him yet, and clearly wanted to use his powers for themselves.

Diplomacy, that was what was needed. His mother always said he could talk his way out of anything. He let out a sigh. Thinking about his family back home made him sad. They would be worrying about him now. Although maybe one or two would hope he was gone for good.

Lucky to still be alive, he reflected. *Unlucky to have been found by wolves*. Only one of them, the young one, had looked at him with a dragon's curiosity and intelligence. Maybe that one would help him. He peered at her as she slept. But what could one small *fliffer-hoffer* do against a whole selfish pack?

CHAPTER 8

Rain thrashed down outside the cracks in the walls of the high chamber in Howling Rock that had been dubbed 'Dragon Cave'. It was a miserable afternoon.

Rana tossed and turned on the rocky floor, unable to sleep for long without the warmth of her pack around her. How was she supposed to sleep without somewolf's paw in her ribs or a tail in her eye? Already, she regretted her decision. A bolt of lightning chased crazy shadows around the room.

Then a crash of thunder woke the dragon with a jolt. It raised itself on one claw and then slumped down again.

With greenish eyes under heavy lids, it peered through the gloom as if seeing nothing.

'I'm here,' said Rana, springing up. 'Don't worry, it's just a storm.'

'I'm worse today,' gasped the dragon, its voice a weak whisper. 'It must be a *voovoodra*—I mean, an infection. I—I'm running out of time.'

It could have been the dim light, but Rana noticed that his green scales had faded to a dull grey.

'Is there anything I can do to help?' Rana asked.

'Please . . . if you could fetch me leaves from the *ganath* bush.'

'What's a *ganath* bush?' asked Rana.

'The leaves look like stars,' croaked the dry voice. 'And they smell like the er . . . urine of a goat. Do you know what I mean?'

'Yes, I know it!' said Rana. 'We call it rankweed. It's disgusting.'

'But good for dragons.' The creature gave a feeble cough. 'Go fast, I beg you!'

Rana was already halfway out the door.

'Where are you going, yearling?' asked Boulder, who was sitting guard outside the entrance to Howling Rock.

'Dragon business,' shouted Rana and vanished into the rainy afternoon.

She returned, sopping wet, with a big bunch of the leaves in her mouth. The taste was horrible, and she spat them gratefully on the floor, then shook her coat free of the excess water.

The dragon extended his neck, and in a slow, deliberate way, began munching the leaves.

Rana watched anxiously as he ate. After a while, she noticed that his breathing was a little easier, even if his colour was still sickly.

'Did that help?' she asked. 'I wasn't sure whether to pre-chew them for you.'

'I'm sorry?'

'You know, eat and regurgitate?'

The dragon pulled a face. 'Don't be disgusting,' he said. 'Are you trying to make me more ill?'

'It's what mother wolves do to feed their cubs sometimes.'

'Ugh. Too much information!'

Rana was surprised. Sometimes the dragon spoke just like a yearling wolf. Almost . . . jokey. Was he really not much different from her?

He reached out a claw and drew the last of the leaves to him. 'Please—find more!'

The dragon had slept for almost a day. Leaders from the Seven Fangs came and went to look in on it. Lupey brought some deer for Rana to eat. Karla had been banned for fear she might harm the dragon, and could sometimes be heard below arguing with Boulder.

At last, the creature stirred.

'Water,' he croaked.

Rana went to the pool on the ground level. She brought water back, in a hollowed-out gourd, carried carefully by its thick stalk in her front teeth. After a drink, the dragon gazed ahead, blinking as if trying to focus on her.

'Thank you,' he said. 'Ow!'

Rana jumped back. 'What's wrong?'

'There's a *pibble*—a mouse in here. Every time it scurries over me, my tail twitches, swishing against the rocks. And I'm already bruised and cut from my crashlanding.' He gave a lop-sided smile. 'Never mind, I'll get used to it.'

Rana eyed the creature, pitifully. She felt helpless, unable to make anything better.

'Why do you sometimes use funny words?'

The dragon's eyes brightened at the question.

'I speak the First Tongue, like all creatures. But over the centuries, we dragons have invented a whole lot more words of our own. Sometimes I slip into Dragonish.' And with that, he shut his eyes once more. For a while, Rana did not move. She simply stood looking at that great scaly beast, trapped in a rock cage not much bigger than itself.

'Are you out of your mind?'

Sly loomed over Rana. She had gone down to the Chamber of the Seven Fangs to find her father, and met the chief of Stalker pack, instead.

'N-no,' said Rana. She was scared of Sly and practically lowering her body into the ground in her politest, most submissive pose.

A group of the fast wolves used as runners gathered around, eager to hear about the dragon.

Silver padded out of the shadows. 'Let that monster out of its cage?'

'Um . . . yes,' she managed at last. 'The dragon is still sick. And he won't get well if he's scrunched up in a miserable dark corner. If we let him out of his cage, he'll still be trapped in the cave, now the entrance is half-blocked.'

'Nonsense,' snorted Sly. 'We've got him where we want him. Never let an enemy up once he's in your jaws. Remember that, yearling.'

Suddenly, Rana forgot all the wolves around her and felt only her frustration.

'He will die if we don't look after him, and that's that!' She picked up a piece of rankweed she had brought with her and held it up in her front paws. 'See this? He needs lots more of it. It'll make him better. But I can't get enough just on my own. Send some runners now to bring back as much as they can!'

Sly and Silver exchanged a glance.

'It can have all the smelly weed it wants,' said Sly, somewhat begrudgingly. 'Lightfoot, get your team onto it.'

Lightfoot sprang up eagerly. 'At last, something for the runners to do! Come on, team, we've got dragon business.'

Silver watched the runners rush out with approval.

'You see?' he said. 'Having a dragon is good for morale. It will unify the Great Pack.'

'Thank you,' said Rana, feeling drained.

Sly was giving her the beady eye. 'Listen, yearling,' he growled. 'We want that dragon to do some magic for us. Something to prove its worth. It has just one week to impress us, or . . .' He pretended to rake his claws across his own throat.

CHAPTER 9

Rana gave a soft, almost inaudible whimper as she gazed through a crack in the cave wall at the distant forest, its treetops swaying in the wind. Out there, all her friends and family were hunting, playing, arguing as ever. What were they doing now? She imagined some silly argument between Fenn and their mother, and almost shed a tear.

'So, you are still here, my spokeswolf,' a quiet, croaky voice broke the silence.

Rana turned towards the sprawling creature. Its dark-green claws poked through the front bars as it tried to stretch.

Yes, the dragon's voice was still weak, but it sounded

different somehow. There was a new note in it. A bit of spirit.

'What is your name, little *fliffer-hoffer*?' he asked.

'It isn't fliffer-whatsit. It's Rana.'

'Is that your short name for daily use? I suppose you have many others.'

'No,' Rana replied. 'It's my only name.'

The dragon smiled. 'You are very silly to give me your only name,' he said. 'Some say that telling someone your true name gives them power over you.'

'Wolves don't say that.'

'Ah well, you are not a *kazzikar*—I mean, a sorcerer,' he said. 'Dragon magic makes things complicated. In fact, far too complicated.' He sighed.

'What's your name?' asked Rana.

'Lyricon,' came the reply.

'Haha!' said Rana. 'Why did you tell me *your* name?'

The dragon gave her a look. 'My real name is much longer. In fact, seventeen times longer. That little part of it won't hurt me. I give it away to you freely.'

For a while, the large, scaly creature just lay there, looking around.

'You seem to be feeling a bit better,' she said,

noticing a glimmer of leafy green returning to his scales.

'Yes, the *ganath* did its work.'

Rana hesitated. 'You could have spoken to Silver and the other pack leaders. Why didn't you ask them to bring it to you earlier?' she asked.

'That lot? The *mubbimurkers*? I am always listening to them talking about whether or not I should be killed. I don't trust any of them not to try and poison me.' He lowered his voice. 'You are different,' he said. 'For some reason, I feel like I can trust you.'

These words affected Rana and she stared back at the creature as if transfixed.

Lyricon didn't seem to notice. He continued, 'But now I'm hungry. I've never been so hungry.'

'That's a good sign!' said Rana, remembering what her mother would say.

'*Splog*,' Lyricon added. 'I need *splog*.'

'What's *splog*?'

'Fish. Not just any fish. Not the little bony ones. Something big, like *squallyrook*! That's er . . . salmon. Salmon is good for sick dragons.'

In moments, she was baying down to Lightfoot and the runners below.

'*Squallyrook!*' she shouted. 'I mean, salmon! Get lots of salmon. This is dragon business!'

Lyricon popped the last salmon in his mouth and pulled it by the tail as he sucked all the flesh off its bones. Then he threw the tail away.

'Thank you. I'll soon be feeling a lot better,' he said. 'Another nap, and—'

'I don't know if you have time for a lot of naps,' said Rana. 'Now you've perked up, I've got some news for you.'

Rana explained about how the pack leaders expected Lyricon to work some magic for them.

His face fell. 'Well, I can't breathe fire at the moment. The sickness has put out my spark, and it will take a long time to come back. And if they want some other demonstration of dragon power, they will have to let me out of the cage,' said Lyricon. 'Because I need sun on my wings to do magic.'

'Really?'

'Yes, a *kazzikar*—a sorcerer dragon gets his magic power through the sun. I have none at all in this gloomy corner. Go and tell them that!'

*

'I cannot believe my ears!'

Rana was in the Chamber of the Seven Fangs. All of the chief wolves were there.

'Lyricon said he needs sunlight on his wings—'

'And you believed him?'

Sly and Silver enjoyed a horrible snorting laugh at her expense.

'Rana, you are really very gullible,' said Silver. 'I'm surprised your family brought you up that way.' Here, the old wolf looked at Darkmane, who had an aloof, dignified air.

'Get Karla!', snapped Sly. 'The old she-wolf is always around here somewhere.'

There was howling and scampering about in the outer passages, and soon Karla appeared, wary and narrow-eyed. Her presence seemed to quieten the pack chiefs a little. Rana was delighted to see her.

'How are they treating you, little one?'

'Don't call me that!' whispered Rana.

'Silence!' barked Sly. 'Now, Storyteller, in all the old tales, did you ever hear of a dragon needing sunshine on its wings to do magic?'

'No,' said Karla. 'But there's a good one about them burning a wolf empire down—'

'We know that one,' grunted Sly.

There was a moment's pause. Rana tried to catch Karla's eye.

'You're not helping!' Rana whispered.

'And you are?' Karla replied.

'Would you,' croaked Sly, 'release a dragon from its cage just to see if it really did need sunshine on its wings to do magic?'

'No,' Karla replied. 'I might release it if it promised never to come back again, but not for much else.'

The Seven Fangs all looked at each other. Silver drew himself up to his full height.

'It is the decision of this council that the dur-a-gon will not be let out of its cage. We expect some magic in three days' time.'

Rana was dismayed. 'Well, that's just made everything worse and even more impossible! What am I supposed to do now?'

She had aimed her remark at Karla, but the echoes of the chamber made it sound like she was addressing everybody.

'Go away and do what you're told,' said Sly. 'Darkmane, I'm surprised your daughter has the insolence to speak to her betters in that way.'

Darkmane looked proud. 'It's the way she was brought up,' he said.

'Well, that's that,' croaked Lyricon, flopping his long body down in a dismal attitude, his tail poking out of the stalactite bars at one end and his long snout and flared nostrils peering out through the other.

'No sunlight, no magic,' he continued.

'They thought it was a trick,' said Rana. 'Was it a trick, just to get out? I never thought of that.'

'No, it wasn't!' said Lyricon with indignation. 'Where do these *mubbimurkers* get the idea that dragons are lying, evil monsters that need locking up?' He sounded genuinely dismayed.

'It's in our old stories,' said Rana. 'Dragons destroy the world of the wolves with fire.'

Lyricon sighed. 'Oh well, yes. I'm afraid we are a bit like that—some of us, anyway.'

'And you blasted fire at me when we found you.'

Lyricon's face fell. 'I apologise. It was supposed to be a warning shot.'

'A warning shot?' replied Rana, feeling her ruined mane with a back paw. 'Well, thanks for the warning.'

'Still, you have been touched by dragonfire and

survived,' said Lyricon. 'That is . . . remarkable. You are obviously a special wolf.'

Rana looked up in surprise. For a while, silence fell upon the chamber.

'Karla said she had never heard of dragons needing sunshine to do magic,' Rana said.

'We don't exactly advertise it. It's a weakness we prefer our enemies not to know.'

'So, why did you tell me?'

'This is life or death, isn't it!' blurted out the dragon with sudden passion. 'What am I supposed to do?'

Lyricon lay in a forlorn attitude, peering at her through one half-closed eye. He looked like he had already given up. On the other side of the cave, the sun had risen, but its pale beams only touched a few parts of the floor, out of the reach of the dragon.

'I'll go and talk to the chiefs again.' Rana sighed.

But when she went down below, the Chamber of the Seven Fangs was empty. She found her mother organising the new dens at the foot of the Rock.

'Your father told me all about you telling the council off for not helping that creature. I was so proud.'

'Do you agree with me about freeing the dragon?'

'Well, I don't know about *that*, but I do think the chiefs need taking down a peg or two.'

Fenn appeared and almost knocked Rana over with an enthusiastic bound to greet her. 'Come on, Rana,' he said. 'You're always stuck up in that cave. You must be bored silly. Let me show you the dens!'

With a sigh, Rana followed Fenn around Howling Rock. Families from all the other packs were moving into the hollows at the bottom of the great stone pinnacle.

'Look, this one has the cubs from Cowbird pack, they're hilarious—none of them have any manners. And yesterday, a family from Lightning pack fought with a family from Horizon pack for the quietest den at the back. They were all bellowing loudly about how quiet they wanted it to be. That was hilarious too. I nearly had to go in personally and sort it out. I—' Fenn stopped. 'You look sad, Ranny, what's up?'

Rana explained about the dragon needing some sunshine. Fenn continued to look at the cubs playing.

'Can't you get sunshine from somewhere else?' he asked vaguely.

'Sorry, what?' Rana frowned.

His attention elsewhere now, her brother had leapt up onto a rock and was poised as if about to join in the rough and tumble with the Cowbird cubs.

'Oh, that's good, Fenn,' Rana remarked. 'Get sunshine from somewhere else, other than the sun where all the sunshine comes from!'

Fenn shrugged. 'Just an idea.'

'You're hopeless!' she barked and turned back.

CHAPTER 10

The rain poured down. Even if Lyricon could get out of his cage, he wouldn't be able to bask in any sunlight, Rana reflected. He just stared into space, his tail drooping and his every scale looking almost as grey as the sky. Rana found herself drifting off to sleep.

In her dreams, a butterfly flew by. It had a familiar spiral shape on its wings. She followed it to a flowery grove where Karla was telling a story. It was *The Little Sunbeam*. She liked this story, one of the more magical ones. A little sunbeam wanted to stay and see what the world was like after the sun went down. So it hid in a beautiful crystal where—

Rana woke up. She sprang to her feet and raced to the cave exit.

'Where are you going in such a hurry?' asked Lyricon.

'Just an idea,' she replied.

In moments, she was giving orders to Lightfoot and the other runners.

'What is going on?' asked Darkmane. Rana was greeting runners as they came back from various tracks in the wilds, bringing any crystals they could find with them.

'Maybe nothing,' Rana said.

'Doesn't look much like "nothing" to me,' said Darkmane.

Misty, from Snowfoot pack, dropped several large amethysts from her jaws.

'There are lots of these at Shining Creek in the North Pass,' she said. 'My family is fetching more.'

Just then, Fenn came by and dropped some bright-blue opals at her feet. 'I've heard about the crystal hunt,' he said, grinning. 'I'm joining in too. What is it, some kind of prank?'

'No,' said Rana. 'It's an idea *you* had. Help me

with these.' And she began carrying the crystals up to the Dragon Cave.

Lyricon awoke from a gloomy doze to see a pile of sparkling gems in front of his nose.

He raised a single eyebrow. 'A present?'

His droll air, even in the face of imminent disaster, again reminded Rana of the jokey style of the younger wolves. How could this dragon really be so bad?

'I'm trying to help you,' she said. 'We wolves have a story. A sunbeam wants to stay on earth, so it hides in a crystal. In the bigger story it plays hide and seek with the moon, but that's not important.'

Lyricon looked tired and gazed rather dimly at the gems. He tapped a pointy claw on his bars, a little habit he had acquired.

'And what *is* important?'

'There could be sunlight trapped in these gems,' she said. In the face of the big, gloomy dragon, her inspiration seemed a bit wild. Distant thunder rumbled. Lyricon continued to stare.

'You've gone very quiet,' she said.

'Push them through the bars,' he replied. The sparkles seemed to have put a small glint in his eye.

He put the palm of his right front claw over the biggest gem, a purple amethyst.

'Do you know,' he murmured, 'we dragons have ancient myths about a group of early sorcerer dragons called Crystalists. No-one really knows how they did it, but . . .' he began muttering to himself. He was now clasping the amethyst in both palms, his brow furrowed.

'Get more,' he said.

Rana heard her name being called as she carried another jaw-load of crystals up to the Dragon Cave.

What now? She really didn't have time for interruptions. Running back down to the entrance of Howling Rock, her spirits rose as she saw Ayala, and with her, Fenn. Behind them, runners were dropping more and more sparkling stones all the time.

'I've had a word with Darkmane,' said her mother, 'and it's obvious the chiefs have put too much on you,' she said. 'Fenn is going to be your helper. 'He's not to pester the dragon, and he is to do everything you say.'

Rana grinned. 'Everything I say? Alright, Fenn, stand on your head.'

'I'll stand on *your* head,' Fenn replied.

'There you are,' said Ayala. 'A masterpiece of cooperation. The dream team.'

It was with a much lighter heart that Rana went scampering back to her spokeswolf duties, her cheeky brother at her heels.

In Dragon Cave, Lyricon was pulling crystals through the bars of his cage and studying them in the pale moonlight.

'This is my brother, Fenn,' said Rana. 'He's a yearling like me, and he wants to help too. The crystals were partly his idea,' she added.

'Hey, Dragon!' said Fenn, with the breezy manner he would have used with any yearling.

Rana smiled. Her brother was really not the type to be awed by a magical creature from the Far-off Times.

Lyricon raised one green eyebrow. 'Hmm. Another *fliffer-hoffer*, I see.' He yawned, showing off razor-sharp fangs.

'Fenn can be a bit annoying—' Rana batted her brother with a paw as he opened his mouth to whine in protest. 'But at least he's not a *mubbimurker*. I hope you'll both get along.'

Lyricon gave the slightest nod of greeting to Fenn, then returned to his work as if nothing had happened.

It was now night. Rana was looking at the improbable sight of a dragon, over three times her size, lying on his back with crystals piled onto his eyelids.

'Have you gone to sleep?' she asked. At first, he did not reply. Then he spoke quietly.

'They are bringing power back into my eyes,' he said. 'You were right. There is sunlight trapped in most of these crystals. And from the feel of it, some of it is ancient sunlight, refracted deep into the heart of the gems. You know, the old sorcerer Kazikle said that a crystal's heart goes on forever.'

Rana pulled one of the amethysts towards her with a paw, and stared into it. She gazed deeply, searching for the ancient sunlight. As she did, the stiffer fur of her scorched mane seemed to stir and tingle at its roots. The sensation made her whole body feel more alive.

'I-I can sort of sense something,' she said. 'Like a tickle in my mane.'

'Hmm . . .' said Lyricon. 'That is very interesting. In very rare cases, they say those who are touched by the dragonfire of a sorcerer—and survive—can develop a special . . . awareness.'

He cupped the gems in his paws and sat up, the roof of the cage making him hunch a little.

'W-what does it all mean?' Rana asked.

As he opened his claws, a soft glow spiked up from the crystals, bathing them in a pale rosy light.

'It means magic,' he replied.

CHAPTER 11

It was dawn. A robin could be heard whistling in the grey shadows of the canyon outside. The first rays of the sun were sparking answering gleams from the pile of crystals that were now surrounding Lyricon in his cage.

The dragon had one day to produce some magic. Or else. Neither Rana nor Lyricon felt the need to mention this fact. Fenn gnawed on an elk shinbone in the background.

'Just look at it all!' breathed Rana, the straggly fur on her scorched mane seeming to stand on end. 'The chamber is making my fur twitch already.'

The dragon looked up. 'You really feel the magic,

don't you? That is promising!' He held up a topaz and studied its sheen with an expert eye. 'The gems here are full of ancient sun power. There must be something special about this area,' he said. 'But right now, that's not our concern. We need to do some magic.'

Rana pointed her nose at some blue sapphires, twinkling like stars in the early-morning light. 'I've noticed while moving them that I get more of a tingle from these smaller, deep-coloured crystals, than the bigger ones,' she said.

'I'll put them all together,' said Lyricon. He began to arrange them into a circle just inside the bars of his cage.

'Now, I need to get those grumpy old wolves on my side, quickly,' he said. 'Is there anything that wolves particularly like to eat?'

'Meat, of course!' said Rana.

'In that case, I'll bring them a little treat.' He stared into a big red crystal. 'I'm seeing bison as my best bet,' he said. 'The crystal is resonating with the presence of one nearby. They'll like that, won't they? Fetch the *mubbimurkers* now!'

Rana dashed off. In moments, she had returned to

the Dragon Cave with Sly, Darkmane and Silver on her heels.

'Is that the best you could do?' asked Lyricon, with a little smile. 'I want a big audience for this!'

Lyricon lay behind the bars of his cage, his head propped up on his front claws, staring into the pile of gems before him.

'Get on with it, then,' growled Sly.

Lyricon made a few gestures and appeared to be muttering words. For a moment, nothing happened, then the dawn light in the cave flickered and went out. Darkness surrounded them. Little sparks began to dance in the air above the gem pile.

'Is—is it safe?' asked Silver in a querulous tone.

'My daughter is here,' said Darkmane. 'And she is unafraid.'

'It's safe,' whispered Rana, her eyes glowing with expectation. 'Prepare for a treat . . .'

There was a flash, a tiny thunderclap and a vile smell like swamp gas.

The wolves stared. There, floating in the air before them, was a bison skull. Narrow, pale and split with age, it had one broken horn, and a spider nesting in one eye socket.

As they all gaped, it dropped to the floor, tipped to one side and fell over. The spider ran away.

Sly broke the silence. 'Bah!' he said. 'It didn't even have any meat on it.'

Lyricon had his face buried in his hands. '*Drabble!*' he cursed. 'I wanted bison, and this mouldy old skull must have been buried near here!'

'It *was* magic,' said Darkmane.

'Yes,' yelped Rana, wide-eyed. 'And think what it shows we can do!'

'It just makes me feel hungrier than ever.' Silver sighed. 'I enjoy a good bison head.'

'I can see a lot of wasted effort,' said Sly, looking around at all the gems in their dazzling patterns. 'We were promised a treat, and all I see is a sort of silly trick, such as cubs play on All Spirits' Night!'

'A silly trick?' Rana exploded. 'I've been working day and night for this silly trick! Not only did I bring this dragon back from the dead, but I found a way for his magic to work even in that gloomy old cage!' She looked to Lyricon, but there was no help from that direction; he was slumped in disappointment, his face hidden.

Sly rose up and peered down at Rana. 'It is a

reasonable beginning,' he said. 'But nothing else. We expect more.'

'R-reasonable?' Rana spluttered. 'At least say you'll let him out. He can do better magic then.'

'Don't be ridiculous,' said Sly. 'He has done nothing to earn such a gesture.'

'Nothing?' Rana could not believe her ears. 'You have seen actual magic here! He delivered what you wanted to see!'

'You are naïve, Rana,' said Sly. 'You must think of it from *our* point of view, not his.' Here, he glanced across at Lyricon, who was a picture of dejection, his face still buried in his claws. 'We have rushed to his side after a terrible accident. We have given him shelter, constant attention and made him well again.' He walked over to the cage. 'We expect far more than a broken old bison skull. You owe us big time!'

Rana's heart sank down to her paws. Sly's words were those of a wolf that would always believe—no, he would always *know*—he was right about everything. The unfairness filled her with rage. She couldn't let Lyricon die a prisoner because the Stalker pack chief was stubborn and cruel. Something snapped within her. Forgetting her fear of Sly, she flattened her ears and growled.

'How dare you—'

But Darkmane stepped forward to cut her off.

'If we're finished here, Sly, there were some Stalker runners with a message for you.' He looked pointedly at Rana. 'Daughter, you need to go and cool your temper.'

Sly's gaze was still on Rana. He curled his lip in a snarl. 'The dragon gets nothing—yet. We've done a lot for him,' he continued, 'and we expect a lot back. Unless he gives us a miracle by dawn tomorrow, I'll rip his throat out myself.'

A pile of yellow crystals went tumbling as Lyricon's tail accidentally knocked them over.

'It's obviously too cramped in here!' he moaned, his long, serpentine body twisting awkwardly to rearrange the crystals again. 'It didn't matter so much when I was sick and could hardly move. But how can a dragon do magic without waving its claws about or having sun on its wings?'

'They are not ready to let you out,' said Rana. 'Sly made that very clear. He and Silver are the worst.

They don't care about anywolf else. They just won't listen to reason!' Her eyes flashed, and she paced back and forth in front of the dragon's poky cage.

In her heart, Rana knew her anger wasn't helping. Finally, she stopped pacing, took a deep breath and sat back on her haunches.

'Life is always tough, but we are tougher,' she said at last.

Lyricon raised an eyebrow. 'We are?'

'It's what my mother says when things get me down,' she added. 'We'll get tough now. You've already managed a bison skull, and with my help, you'll do something even more magical. Forget the cage, forget Sly, forget it being hard. Let's just do it. Let's create a really big miracle. Then they'll have to let you out.'

'Will they?' Lyricon did not look hopeful. His tail was flopping like a dead plant, and the spines along his back also had a wilted look.

'Listen,' said Rana. 'I noticed before that when we had all the most powerful gems together, the magic was a bit too strong, hard to control. I could feel it in my fur. But when you put, say, one red opal after three sapphires, the power calms down. It's still there but sort of channelled—like when you put rocks into a stream to control the flow.'

Lyricon pulled a face. 'I never put rocks into a stream.'

'I think it's about patterns,' Rana said. 'Anyway, I want to try it. If we mix the powerful stones and the less powerful in the right way . . .'

The pair talked and worked long into the night. Lyricon's dexterous claws moved faster and faster as his eyes brightened. As the night deepened, the gems began to glow softly, like a constellation of stars in the chamber.

'A rabbit!'

'Hardly worth chasing!' yawned Ela. Starlight pack, including an off-duty Fenn, were resting on the grassy slopes near Howling Rock when dawn broke.

'It's mine!' Fenn said. 'I could use a snack right now.'

He broke away from the woodland cover and chased the little jackrabbit up the side of the hill. With a sigh, Ela followed. Riki jumped up too.

Gripper groaned. 'I suppose I'd better go and make sure they don't get into any trouble.'

With Gripper in pursuit of the yearlings, several other Starlight wolves followed suit. The rabbit proved a tricky adversary, jumping, twisting and changing direction. Trying to do the same, Fenn tripped over his tail and landed on his snout. He heard Gripper chuckle behind him.

'The rabbit is yours, is it? It doesn't seem to know that!'

'It's almost as if the poor bunny doesn't *want* to be eaten,' said Ela, with a smile.

With its fluffy tail bobbing up and down behind it, the rabbit raced over the top of a ridge, with Fenn close behind. Then he came to a halt so quickly that Gripper almost crashed into him.

'What are you playing at?' Gripper shouted. Then he fell silent.

Over the ridge was Fern Valley, usually a quiet nook with just a clear stream running through it. Now, filling that valley was the biggest herd of white-tailed deer they had ever seen. Nudging Fenn with his shoulder, Gripper quickly led the wolves out of sight.

'We've got something else for the pack to hunt now!' he said.

It was the biggest deer feast the wolves had ever known. Gripper quickly sent a runner to the Seven Fangs, and the packs spent the day hunting in shifts. By twilight, the Great Pack was as well fed as even Karla could ever remember. There had been so many deer that a great many had now fled, or been allowed to escape, so that the pack would have plenty of future prey.

Across the evening, more and more wolves kept arriving to share the feast. Darkmane, Sunstreak and Silver came to the great feed as night fell. A smaller wolf came trotting behind them.

'Rana!' Gripper cried out and bounded over to meet her. 'We miss you every day! Hard to believe, I know.' He grinned.

'Ha ha,' said Rana. 'You are so stuffed you can hardly move!' The pack gathered round the new arrivals.

'Living the dream,' said Fenn. 'And I found them all by myself.'

Rana looked at Gripper.

'For once,' said Gripper, 'he isn't making it up.'

Ayala was quick to scent the arrival of her daughter. 'Trust you to arrive at dinnertime,' she said.

'Of course.' Rana smiled. 'Life at the top of the Rock hasn't changed me, you know.'

Darkmane and Sly drew Rana aside, as the other wolves partied and feasted under the moon. Karla joined them.

'Now, this was the work of our guest in the cave up top, wasn't it?' said Darkmane.

'Of course,' said Rana. 'We were working on this practically all night.'

'I knew it,' said Sly, pleased with himself. 'The best feast ever. I was so right to put the pressure on!' He trotted off, his bushy tail swishing smugly.

Karla scowled. 'Oh, this is dragon-magic alright,' she said. 'White-tails are not migratory deer. They stay mostly on the slopes of the Wilderland Barrier Range, where the cave lions hunt them. These white-tails would be crazy to come into this narrow valley, where they are easy to catch. It is most unnatural!'

Unnatural . . . the word brought a grey cloud over Rana's happiness. Yes, the deer had been brought somewhere it was very foolish of them to go. But they had no choice with Lyricon's spell. Was magic sometimes cruel, then? It made the success taste a little bitter.

'Unnatural but tasty,' said Darkmane, with a grin. 'Can't you be happy about anything, Grandma?'

'I'm not your grandma!' snapped Karla. 'And yes, I can be happy about something—seeing Rana again.'

'It's good to see you, too.' Rana sighed. 'I miss all of you!'

Darkmane began to head off, and she chased after him.

'Dad?'

'Yes?' the Starlight chief peered down at her.

'The dragon can't stay in that cage any longer,' Rana said, her eyes bright. 'We've done everything the Seven Fangs wanted. Can you talk to Sly and the others? If Lyricon stays in there much longer, I think he will go crazy. I'm not kidding.'

Darkmane was thoughtful. 'Well, we don't want a crazy dragon on our hands. I will talk to the other chiefs,' he said. 'But don't get his hopes up.'

Karla overheard this and scowled. 'I hope that dragon isn't enchanting you,' she said.

'He's really not bad—for a dragon,' said Rana. 'I think we've been lucky.'

'I hope so,' came the reply.

CHAPTER 12

'You have served us well, Dragon,' said Silver. 'And after some consideration, we have decided to reward you.'

He gave a nod. At this, six of the strongest wolves sprang into action, and with all their might, shouldered the heavy rocks, one by one, away from the end of the stalactite cage.

Rana watched, half pleased, half anxious, as Lyricon slowly slithered out of the cramped space, making for the area of the cave wall where cracks let in narrow sunbeams. He began stretching his limbs with evident relief. Scales that had seemed grey now glittered emerald green in the light.

Slowly standing on his hind legs, and stooping to avoid the low roof, Lyricon was taller than a grizzly but less bulky, more sinuous. A leathery wing unfurled, its dark skin shimmering in the morning light like a holly leaf. The other, injured, wing remained held close to his side.

There was a murmur of appreciation and some wagging of tails.

'Dragon, do you have anything to say?' asked Sunstreak.

'I thank you for saving my life and granting me this small freedom,' Lyricon said. He attempted an awkward bow. 'I promise to do even better magic to show my appreciation to the Great Pack.'

'You'd better,' said Sly. 'I'm picturing never-ending herds of tasty bison. No matter how many you catch, more keep coming.'

'Excellent idea,' said Silver. 'Work on that right away.'

And with that, the chief wolves departed.

When their pawsteps had receded, Lyricon hobbled stiffly around Dragon Cave, peering through the cracks in the walls. At first, he winced a little every time he moved.

'They've let me out, but I'm still a prisoner,' he said after a while. 'I'm too big to fly out of any of these windows, and you'll notice they've shoved a couple of extra boulders at the entrance to stop me squeezing out.'

'Yes,' said Rana. 'But it's a step forward. You'll be able to put your wings in the morning sun. And you can move about now. I hoped you'd be happy.'

'I am happy. I'm super-duper-wooper happy. But I've no idea how to make an endless herd of bison. That's Eternity Magic. Borderline impossible.'

'Don't say that,' said Rana. 'Look at what we've done together already. I think we can do anything. I'll send out runners for more crystals immediately!'

'There you are,' said Fenn, dropping an enormous purple amethyst in the centre of the cave. 'I carried it all the way back from Pine Top without choking—which Gripper didn't think I could do. I don't actually think we can fit any more gems in here now!'

Rana admired their work. The chamber was unrecognisable from the previous day. Glistening piles of golden topaz, sky-blue sapphires and dazzling, rainbow-hued opals were everywhere.

'Let's make some magic,' said Lyricon, the sparkling stones clearly brightening his mood. 'Now, how do we create that endless herd?'

'We?!' Rana laughed. '*You* know all the spells.'

'Yes, but you understand the crystals. You feel their power, thanks to your magic mane. Without you, the deer would never have happened. Without you, I'd be dead.'

'I got lucky,' said Rana. 'I had a dream.'

'Yes, but having the right dream is another sign of magic. You are special, little *fliffer-hoffer!* And you've brought me back to life. Really—you, and you alone. I thought I was in the clutches of enemies until you came along. You gave me hope when I had none.'

It was morning, and a low sun penetrated the morning mist to light up the cave, the gemstones gleaming in its pale rays.

'It's quite nice in here now,' said Lyricon, looking around. 'If I only had some music to work to, it would be just like my sanctum at home.'

'Music?'

'Yes, I always work to music at home. What kind of songs do you like?'

Rana thought for a moment and smiled. 'I

suppose the mockingbird is my favourite—especially its night song. Then there's the thrasher. I mean, for pure melody. But maybe the hermit thrush is my real favourite. Pretty, but a bit sad too. You know, kind of deep?'

Lyricon laughed. 'I was talking about music played by instruments! There's a band I like, back home, called The Dreamons, but . . . well . . . I can't expect a wolf from the wild to understand that.'

'A band?'

'Never mind. Your musical tastes are perfect just as they are. I suppose I shall be a fan of birdsong soon, the longer I sit up here. I do hear an owl occasionally who has a certain flair for creepy effects. We talk sometimes—mainly when I tell him to pipe down.'

While Lyricon was chatty, Rana took the chance to ask him something.

'How did you end up crashing here?' she asked. 'Can you remember?'

'I honestly don't remember.' He sighed. 'My best guess is that I was doing a traveling spell of some sort, and it went wrong. Maybe I got struck by lightning. It can have unpredictable effects on dragon magic. I wonder if my family even know I'm alive.'

Lyricon fell silent. Rana could see his kaleidoscopic eyes had gone shadowy again, and his tail flopped in a listless way.

'Are you OK?' she asked.

'Just tired,' said Lyricon.

'I think maybe you're a bit homesick, too,' she said gently.

Lyricon's scales glinted as he turned to peer through the crack in the wall to the sky outside, but he made no other reply.

Rana looked around at all the piles of crystal in their intricate patterns.

After a while, she spoke again. 'You've been working hard recently,' she said. 'Maybe you just need a rest after all that magic.'

He sighed. 'A rest would be nice. A chance to heal my wing, and time to think about how to get home.'

'Is it definitely broken?'

'I wasn't sure before, when I was squashed against the wall in that cage. But now I'm out, I'm pretty positive. It hurts whenever I try to move it.'

'I wonder . . .' said Rana.

'Wonder what?'

'Well, Karla once told me story about a secret pool

with healing powers. I thought it was just an old tale, but with all the magic things I'm seeing now . . .'

Lyricon arched an eyebrow. He began tapping the long claw on his right hand against the floor, as he often did when thinking.

'You could ask her. But why would she help me fix my wing?'

'Because you might promise to fly away and not come back.'

Lyricon grinned. 'She would like that. Maybe it's worth a go.'

'Is flying away what you really want?' Rana asked quietly.

'Of course. Those *mubbimurkers* still discuss the best way to kill me if I turn troublesome. Do you know what that does to my sleep?'

Rana found it hard to meet his troubled gaze.

'I'm sorry about them.' She sighed. 'But look, maybe we can find a magic solution to your wing. Then you could make us all an eternal bison herd and fly off a hero. I'm sure even the *mubbimurkers* would agree that was fair.'

'Well . . .' Lyricon looked encouraged at last. 'Let's make a plan. You'll go and ask Karla about the pool, and I'll have that rest I need. Tomorrow we can see how things look.'

Rana nodded. Inside, she felt a little sad.

'I'll miss you, you know,' she said. 'If you fly away.'

'I'll miss my *fliffer-hoffer* too,' he said. 'At the moment, you're the only friend I've got in the world.'

Then Rana was heading down the tunnels to find Karla. She had a big feeling inside, knowing that a dragon had called her his friend.

Frost Forest
Bear River
Rushing Waters
Pine Top
Long Creek

Part Two:

Sorcerer and Apprentice

CHAPTER 13

A lonely owl hooted somewhere in the night outside. Lyricon gave a deep sigh. He could not even peer at the view tonight; there was no moon, and darkness reigned utterly. He felt like that owl, lonely and lost in the dark. Where, in fact, in all the world was he? Was home really so far away? Was it gone forever? How would he ever know?

He thought of his chamber at home, his scrolls and his music, his soft feather nest. To be honest, he had often been lonely there, too, but at least he hadn't been living under the threat of death.

He tried to waggle his left wing and immediately felt a jolt of pain. Even if he had been well, there was no way he could fly away; those cold-blooded older wolves had trapped him well.

Left completely to himself, he watched a tiny firefly weave its way across the chamber. A spark in the darkness, it cheered his spirits.

'Hey,' he said. 'I can make light too, you know!'

He picked up three of the crystals that best kept and amplified light. Balancing them on top of each other he murmured a few words to spark them into life. A little magic lit them up in a small, pretty display. Outside, the sad-sounding owl hooted again.

'Cheer up, my friend,' said Lyricon. 'There is always some light in the darkness.'

Suddenly, he stopped and stared at his little mound of glowing gems. They had given him an idea.

CHAPTER 14

It had been a wonderful break for Rana. She had visited the dens at the foot of Howling Rock, where Starlight pack were now settled in their new home. She had spent time with her mother, told a few stories to the cubs Scruff and Fluff, and swapped some gossip with Ela and Riki about the other packs.

Karla did not like having a permanent den and would wander the forest for hours as of old. But as the first stars were peeping out, Karla returned to Howling Rock and sat down with Rana.

'The story of the enchanted pool?' the old she-wolf said. 'It is really *The Tale of Firemane the Fierce*. He fought the king of the cave lions to protect his pack, and was so wounded that everywolf believed he had limped off somewhere to die alone. In fact, Firemane had found his way to the enchanted pool deep under Hunter's Reach. He bathed in it and was restored to full strength. Some say he watches over us now.'

'Where is the pool supposed to be?' Rana asked.

'I have no idea,' said Karla. 'When my mother passed the story onto me, she just said it was underground somewhere. I stopped telling that tale, because it made foolish yearlings think they might be saved from injury by a magic pool. Hmph! Wolves save themselves by means of their wit. Why? Did somewolf ask for the tale?'

'No, I was just curious.' Rana tried to hide her disappointment. She wouldn't have much to tell Lyricon, after all.

Thinking about the dragon, she wondered if Lyricon really was OK. Stretching and sitting in the sun for a while had cheered him a little, but he still seemed drained. Maybe he had fallen sick again. She began to feel guilty. Her friend was still a prisoner. And looking after him was her job. It was the one thing the chiefs had asked her to do. She didn't have to join the pack on patrols or look after the cubs anymore—just attend to Lyricon. Perhaps she had been wrong to leave him.

Then she had a bright idea. The rankweed. She would go back to the Rock, creep in so as not to disturb him, and leave Lyricon some rankweed in case he needed it. When he woke up, he would know that she had looked in on him. And she would feel better having done her duty. Giving her mother a goodbye nuzzle, she ran off into the forest before anyone could ask her where she was going.

Darkness was falling and she had a hard time finding some of the foul-smelling weed. They had picked so much of it already! After snuffling around a brook near Kingfisher Creek, she managed to find a clump, and snatched it up into her jaws.

Don't worry, Lyricon, I'm coming.

It was midnight at Howling Rock, and the Seven Fangs were nowhere to be seen. Boulder barely looked up from a bone he was chewing as Rana slipped by. Soft-footed, she scampered up through the passages to Dragon Cave. There were sounds from inside. Not as she had expected—the sound of a dragon snoring—but mutterings and soft clinking noises.

Puzzled, she peered in through the space between the boulders that served as the wolves' entrance. Something was different about the cave. Mud was pasted over the cracks in the walls that acted as windows. Why?

There, at the far side of the chamber, was Lyricon. Not asleep, not looking tired, but hard at work. He had built a tower out of tiny crystals, and somehow all the rocks were sticking together. On top was one big gemstone, a sapphire like a crystal ball.

Something different in Lyricon's air made her keep quiet. Finally, the dragon made a gesture with his claws, spoke some Dragonish word and touched the base of the crystal tower. For a moment nothing happened, then it lit up.

Rana watched, wide-eyed. The light reached the globe at the top of the tower and something amazing happened. It began to send out little rings of light, bright circles that rose to the chamber ceiling, growing bigger and bigger, more and more brilliant, until they vanished into thin air. The effect was dazzling. The whole chamber pulsed with magic.

Rana shrank back. Was this why Lyricon had

blocked the windows, to stop anywolf seeing the incredible lightshow? Why had he hidden such a display? Silently, she slipped away. What was Lyricon doing?

Confused, she ran back to her family den, without looking back.

CHAPTER 15

'We are at war!'

Rana had returned to the Rock the next day, still wondering what to say to Lyricon. Should she come straight out and ask him what he had been making so secretly? Or just tell him about the rather disappointing end to their magic-pool idea? Then that whole question had been blown away by the shock announcement from Boulder, guarding the entrance.

'Get in quick,' he said. 'You're missing it.'

All the chiefs were gathered in the Chamber of the Seven Fangs. The lieutenants and runners were there too. Nowolf blinked an eyelid when Rana joined them. Fenn and Lupey were already hidden away at the back.

'It's true,' said Haze, chief of Horizon pack. 'The Cave Lions are gathering at our east border, in huge numbers.'

'You saw them?'

'I met them—and was lucky to escape with my life!'

'They've never crossed into our territory before,' muttered Silver.

'They're starving and dangerous,' said Haze. 'One of them—Gragh, he called himself—pinned me down before I escaped and gave me an earful. He said their homes in the mountains beyond Wilderland had become desolate, devoid of food.' Haze stopped to lick her wounded flank. She was clearly shaken.

'And?' prompted Darkmane.

'Gragh said it didn't matter because they had heard rumours of a land of plenty—ours—and they were moving in!'

'Moving in?' snarled Sly. 'We'll see about that!'

'We have some time,' said Haze. 'The land is flooded between Wildermere and our border at Snake Trail, and most of their forces are having to pick their way through the swamps.'

'Assemble our fiercest warriors!' said Sly. 'If they are coming from the east, we will lie in wait at Thorny Gap and drive them off. If he is right, they will arrive starving and weak. We are all well fed, and—'

'And going soft,' said Darkmane. 'The dragon has been feeding us too well. We haven't had to hunt properly for days.'

'The dragon!' said Silver. 'Now, there is a thought. Come with me!'

'And these cave lions will surely kill me?' asked Lyricon with a puzzled frown. The Seven Fangs were in Dragon Cave. Rana noticed there was no sign of the miniature gemstone tower from the night before, and that all the mud over the cracks had been scraped away.

'Yes,' said Silver. 'One of the reasons we have kept you secret is that other animals will be jealous and fearful of you. If the cave lions invade, they will take Howling Rock, find you and kill you.'

Lyricon gulped.

'Fear not,' said Silver. 'They will not invade. With a dragon on our side, we are sure to win any war.'

'I cannot fight,' said Lyricon. 'My wing is still broken, and after my sickness I don't know if I'll ever be able to breathe fire again. But—'

'But?'

'But I can create something just as good, if used properly: a golem.'

'A golem? What is that?' asked Silver.

'An illusion, or a copy of a dragon,' Lyricon said. 'Something to put terror into your foes. Yes, I believe I can do it. I can even give it a few tricks to do. Come back at midnight and I will show you.'

'You have until sundown!' snapped Sly. There was a general murmur of approval as the council wolves departed.

'More salmon,' said Lyricon, as he started piling crystals. Rana, glad to forget her doubts about him, rushed off to put in the order.

'What news?' growled Sly. Skip and Lightfoot had just returned, exhausted and covered in mud, from a spying run to the east territory.

'The cave lions have made it through the swamp,' said Lightfoot. 'And there are more on the way. We could see them through the mist. They must be really desperate to be making that journey. Maybe the crocs will get a couple of them. But they are going to be no picnic to fight.'

'We should have seen this coming,' said Haze. 'We haven't been patrolling that area so much lately, because—'

'Because we've all been lying around eating deer,' said Sly. 'We can't hang back any longer—we need action, now. I'll stir that dragon up a bit!'

With a bound, Sly leapt onto the boulder in the doorway of Dragon Cave. Looking around, he saw Lyricon sitting at the far end, apparently asleep. A pyramid of gemstones was at his feet. Rana and Fenn lay flat, looking on silently.

'What's going on?' barked Sly. 'You're supposed to be hard at work up here, not having a sleep-in!'

Rana turned. 'Shush, you'll—'

'Wake him up?' asked Sly. 'You're howling right I'll wake him up.'

'Don't!'

Sly leapt down in front of Lyricon, nudging a pile of gems and toppling the big red crystal balanced at the top. There was a blinding flash. Sly was staring down at the fallen crystal. A tiny dark shape was arising from it, like a dark flower blooming.

'You broke his trance!' Rana said.

Out of the crystal rose a shadow in dragon shape. It had no scales, just a grey, ghostly form. Its face had two dark eyes, deep pits devoid of life.

'It wasn't time!' cried Rana.

'W-what?' Lyricon spluttered, in a daze.

'By the claws of Fera!' gasped Sly, as the shadow seemed to fill the room.

It loomed over Sly and spoke in a voice so deep and hollow it seemed to come from beyond the grave. '*Attack . . . enemy!*'

The golem breathed out a deep-blue smoke at Sly. Sly's body seemed to freeze stock still, then it vanished into nothing.

'*Attack . . . enemy!*' said that unearthly grating voice again. The golem flew towards the exit, its shadowy form squeezing easily through the gap.

'No!' cried out Lyricon. 'I hadn't finished the obedience protocols!'

Silver came bounding up to Dragon Cave and met the golem coming down.

'Enemy!' came the word like distant thunder. In a

moment, Silver was swallowed up in clouds of blue smoke.

'W-what's this?' he gasped. Then, *pop!* He was gone.

'It's gone berserk!' cried Rana. 'What are we going to do?' She saw Fenn looking strangely calm, his eyes narrowed.

'Weird!' he said. 'It's not setting off my Scent power at all!'

At the bottom of the Rock, the thing emerged from the entrance, its cold, empty eyes scouring the land. With a yelp, Lightfoot and Skip dashed away as fast as they could. The golem spread its dark wings and flew into the air, then swooped upon a crowd of warrior wolves, newly summoned by the council.

'Do something!' gasped Rana, peering down from Dragon Cave. With horrible cries, five warrior wolves disappeared in smoke.

'Help me!' cried Lyricon, stumbling around in a panic. He was smashing down every crystal pyramid he could find. 'Break the patterns!'

In a mad rush, Rana and Fenn found any crystals that had been put in special rows, and jumped on them, scattering them into disorder. Then, with a mighty heave, Lyricon took the main crystal that the golem had emerged from and hurled it out of the narrow window.

There was a shattering crash. The golem froze in mid-flight—then vanished.

'I must say, that was a very good demonstration,' said Sly, looking pleased. 'Your face!' He chuckled at Rana. 'I was still in the chamber, but invisible,' he said.

'As was I,' said Silver. 'I was hit by magic smoke on the way up, and when I arrived no-one could see me.'

'I knew it,' said Fenn. 'I sensed it wasn't real danger. No-one listened, of course.'

Lyricon sat with his face in his claws. 'The spell was not ready!' he cried. 'You ruined it!'

'Nevertheless,' said Silver. 'Now the panic is over, we are forced to admit it was a great illustration of the terror this golem of yours can cause.'

'It has no lasting powers,' explained Lyricon. 'Just a couple of party tricks. All the advantage is in the effect.'

'Just tricks? Invisibility!' Silver smiled. 'Even brief invisibility could be very useful.'

'You can make another, yes?' asked Sly.

Lyricon still had his claws over his face. He peeped through them at the ruins of his spell-chamber. Rana could tell he was upset.

'Yes, we can,' she said. 'Give us till dawn.'

Wearily, Rana pushed a large block of quartz into place in one of Lyricon's designs. The slow process of rebuilding the magical patterns was underway.

'Ah yes, I feel the magic building up already,' said the dragon. 'Your feeling for Crystal Magic is unerring!'

Rana smiled. She began to nudge some small sapphires into position.

'It's nice to be trusted to do these things,' she said. 'I'm still young—and small for a wolf—and in the pack I am never really chosen to do anything. All the bigger, noisier wolves get chosen.'

Lyricon smiled. 'Perhaps that's why we get on,' he said. 'I am actually quite small for a dragon. And not really fierce at all—'

'Apart from burning my mane off.'

'Apart from that.' He gave an ironic grin. 'It's why I studied sorcery. It gives me a value among my kind.

And saves me from having to do more warrior-like things!'

Rana stopped her work and stared at him, surprised. 'So, can't all dragons do magic?'

'Oh no,' said Lyricon. 'We can all fly and make fire, but complicated sorcery is mainly for nerds like me.'

Rana laughed. She pushed some beautiful rose quartz into place around the sapphires. 'In my pack, we have this thing we call "show of strength",' she said. 'Even if you're scared or useless, you have to learn to act brave to help the pack. I'm not very good at that, so they make fun of me.'

Lyricon helped her put the final pieces into his grand golem pattern.

'I think you have a lot of strength, but you maybe don't like showing it. Or showing off. We're a bit different there—I'm a terrible show-off,' he said. And they both laughed as he prepared the spell.

Rana and Fenn hid behind Lyricon's broken wing. Fur was almost flying as the Seven Fangs raved and rowed.

'Invasion or no invasion,' growled Sly. 'The

dragon must stay in his cave. He cannot be released to control the golem.'

'You will not control it, Sly!'

'Neither will you, Silver!'

'Enough!'

Rana had never heard Darkmane roar so loudly. 'This is getting us nowhere. Why don't we ask Lyricon to decide?'

'He is our slave, not our advisor,' said Sly.

'In matters of magic,' said Sunstreak, 'we are all his pupils.'

All eyes turned to Lyricon. The dragon curved his long tail protectively around the tallest pile of crystals and surveyed the room with disdain.

'I have no desire to enter this battle myself, as I still cannot fly, am unable to blow fire, and do not wish to be ripped apart in a barbaric war of smelly furballs.'

The wolves settled down, quietly glad that Lyricon had not sought to push his own cause.

'I can think of only one wolf right for the job,' said Lyricon, 'and that is Rana.'

'Rana?' exploded Sly. 'A cub?'

'Only she understands my magic,' the dragon

replied. 'In fact, without her, there would be no magic at all.'

Rana felt immensely proud to hear this, but her heart was beating fast.

'Plus, she is a not a cub,' said Darkmane. 'She is a yearling. She is also a storyteller—Karla says so. And remember, this golem is a trick—a sort of story we are fooling the cave lions with.'

'I agree,' said Chiggers, the Cowbird chief. 'Rana deserves our respect. She has been doing a dangerous job, cub-sitting this green monster for two weeks.'

'Thank *you*,' muttered Lyricon.

'Anything is better than Silver calling the shots,' said Sly. 'And I want to be ripping cave lions apart, not playing at magic.'

After some half-hearted grumbling from Silver—who had rather fancied himself as golem master—Rana was accepted in the role. She glanced over at Lyricon and realised that, once again, everyone was looking at her. Would she ever get used to being the centre of attention?

This time, the big dragon shadow did not go on a rampage. Rana watched in quiet awe as it rose slowly upwards. The golem looked imposing, but also very dignified with its wings folded neatly back behind it.

Is this what Lyricon would look like if he was completely well? wondered Rana. *A rather noble, imperious creature?*

'You will obey the she-wolf Rana,' Lyricon was saying in a low, droning voice. 'Look into her eyes.'

Rana felt an icy chill as she stared into those empty sockets of shadow.

'How will I talk to it?' she asked.

'In your head,' said Lyricon. 'Like telling it a story about itself. Tell it now that it is flying around the room.'

Rana had seen the golem flying and found it easy to describe. In her mind, she told the golem how magnificent it looked in flight, with its vast wings beating heavily. She told it how all its muscles worked powerfully together to make it an unstoppable force. The creature of shadow began to come to life.

'Good, good,' said Lyricon. 'Your storytelling is making it very realistic! No foe will guess it is just an illusion.'

Fly, fly! Rana commanded, trying to speak with her mind. The dragon shape rose up on its vast wings—

and went straight through the ceiling. There was no damage to either, as the golem was made of shadow. Rana panicked and brought the golem straight down. This time it went straight into the floor, where it stayed with only a rather glum-looking head peeping out.

'Very good,' said Lyricon, with a smile. 'But you are much too excitable with your new toy. Don't get carried away. Have you ever heard the phrase "less is more"?'

'No.'

'Well, when piloting a golem, less is more. Don't crash it around the place. Make it slow and menacing. You will terrify your foes. You're already terrifying me.'

Rana looked to Fenn for approval.

'You're a natural,' he said. 'But I don't think I'll ever understand this dragon-talk,' he added with a bemused look. 'I mean, how can less be more?'

CHAPTER 16

'Run for your life!'

Skip and Lightfoot had been sent to investigate the latest position of the cave lions. They had found the remains of two dead beavers, much chewed, at the old dam by Storm Falls. The whole area was flooded and boggy, and the runners were picking their way carefully through puddles and debris, searching for tracks, when three scraggy, dark shapes sprang out at them from the nearby pines.

The fleet-footed pair quickly outpaced the invaders, who were tired after their long trek. But following Darkmane's orders, Skip and Lightfoot stayed just within sight so that their pursuers could follow them through Thorny Gap. With sharp, steep crags rising on both sides, their foes would be at a disadvantage when they entered the fertile territory of Hunter's Reach.

Darkmane and Sunstreak met the panting runners as they approached the great screen of spiky scrub at the entrance to Thorny Gap.

'With any luck, they'll run right into our trap,' said Darkmane.

'And I'll be ready with my ambush,' said Sly. He and Chiggers trotted off with Gripper and two dozen warrior wolves to get out of sight.

'Where is our secret weapon?' asked Silver.

Rana appeared with Fenn, who was carrying a big blue crystal in his jaws.

'Here!' said Fenn.

'The golem is in there,' said Rana, pointing at the crystal with her snout. The other wolves looked at her with a mixture of awe and unease.

'I suppose you know what you're doing,' said Silver. 'I do hope we have chosen the right wolf for the job. Fera preserve us!'

I hope we have too, thought Rana. She would have given anything to have Lyricon by her side. Suppose the magic went wrong? Then it would be just wolves versus lions, not a situation she wanted the Great Pack to be in.

Twilight was falling and the last birds were calling from the shadowy trees. Through the gloom, Rana could see dark shapes moving far down the forest trail. They looked big, but rather slow and heavy compared to a wolf. Rana had never seen cave lions before and felt a thrill of fascination mixed with a chill of fear.

'Keep cool,' said Silver. 'Let's see how many of them there are.'

The scent of the wolf packs was hidden by the reek coming from the swampy flooded lands.

'I can see . . . at least five distinct prides,' said Silver, a little nervily.

'More cave lions than I can count,' said Haze, who had the keenest eyes.

Rana and Fenn moved closer together. It was terrifying to think of that vast army of hungry invaders coming with the single idea of taking your territory and killing you if they had to. Although she was flanked by older wolves, Rana's hind legs trembled a little, and her heart thumped.

At last, from the advancing ranks, a gaunt yellow-eyed figure stepped forward. Now Rana could see the cave lion up close, she saw it had no mane, and a rather square jaw. It had a grim, solid look, as if made from the rock of the faraway lands it came from. Yet its pale, sandy fur was hanging from a bony frame. Rana had never seen such a dread creature before, an embodiment of hunger and menace.

'I am Gragh, King of the Cave Lions,' he snarled. 'My army has travelled through swamp and crocodile-infested rivers to reach your land. We are hungry, angry and desperate. Our land has been blighted by disaster, and my people will die if we don't take your lands. Step aside or be devoured.'

Darkmane and Sunstreak exchanged a glance. They had not expected so many invaders. Would the plan really work?

Gragh gave a deeply sinister smile. 'I see your fear!' He laughed. 'It is true, then. The wolves of Hunter's Reach have grown soft. This is your last chance. Stand aside or die.'

Darkmane turned his head and nodded at Silver. Silver was positioned further back, among a group of older wolves who were flanking the youngsters, including Rana and Fenn.

'Rana, you're on,' said Silver.

'Greetings, Gragh,' said Darkmane. 'I know you have had a long journey—I can smell it all over you! But this is *your* last chance to leave. Here is our message to you!'

Unseen by the cave lions, Fenn had dropped the crystal he was carrying at Rana's feet. She stared into its depths. She tried to picture the golem appearing, but instead could only see the ferocious, grim invaders in her mind's eye.

Gragh, a little puzzled, looked at Darkmane quizzically. 'Well?' he snapped. 'What message? Surrender, perhaps?' He gave a long, low growl and his army began advancing.

Rana tried again. *Forget where you are*, she told herself. *Imagine you are back in Lyricon's cosy chamber, surrounded by crystals and magic.*

The moment seemed to last forever. The cave lions were now close enough for Rana to see the saliva dripping from their hungry lips.

'Atta—'

Gragh had started to say 'attack', but the word seemed to stick in his throat. All of the cave lions looked up at once as a dark shape loomed over them, a monstrous creature, bigger than the biggest grizzly. Vast jagged wings stretched out on either side. Two chilling night-black eyes stared from above a wide fanged mouth.

'A dragon!' gasped one very old cave lion. 'The legends are true!'

Rana tried to stay calm as she pictured the golem rising up on dark wings, blue smoke pouring from its jaws. *You are ferocious*, she told it. *You are unstoppable! You breathe fire like a volcano and you spread fear everywhere you go!*

'Run!' came a ragged cry.

Gragh was the first to go. The golem's smoke engulfed him, seeming to leave nothing behind. Howls of dismay filled the air.

With a rage she never knew she had in her, Rana pictured the golem devastating its enemies with a remorseless attack, picking out their biggest, most ferocious warriors to smother in belching smoke. In seconds, chaos was in the ranks of their foes.

'Now!' bellowed Sly.

The Great Pack launched its ambush. Warrior wolves leapt from behind the thorny scrub to converge on the fleeing invaders. The air was filled with roars of terror and dismay from the astonished lions. Gripper from Starlight pack and Temper from Stalker led the attack, snapping and tearing at the retreating flanks.

'Keep at them!' Darkmane snarled.

Rana pictured the golem flying in pursuit of their enemies, a monster of vengeance and wrath. All her fear of invasion, of losing her home and her happy life, was turned around into a fierce desire to protect her pack. Suddenly, she felt unbeatable, like she had truly become the golem . . . then, in an instant, it was all over . . .

The light in the crystal died. The great dragon-shadow vanished into the twilight air.

Gragh and his front-line fighters began to pop back into sight as the invisibility wore off. Utterly terrified and confused, they also joined the retreat. In moments, all that was left was a distant yelping and whining, as the Great Pack drove their enemy back through Thorny Gap and into the swamp beyond.

Sunstreak ordered the younger wolves to stay put, away from the action.

'Look!' Fenn nudged Rana. Nearby, a terrified cave lion had fled over the edge of a crag and was lying broken on the rocks beneath.

'What do we do?' asked Rana.

'There is nothing we can do,' said Fenn. 'Not for that one.'

'Come on, let's see!' said Rana. The pair found a way round the foot of the crag, one of the jagged spurs that made up the natural defences of Thorny Gap. The stricken invader was female, quite old, with silver whiskers. Rotten and patchy fur spoke of a hard life in desolate reaches.

'She's trying to say something,' said Rana. The young wolves stepped closer.

'What is your name?' asked Rana.

'Kurloo,' gasped the lion. She tried to raise her head but could only twist it painfully. 'We didn't want to come here,' she said. 'But our land was cursed. Without any warning, the white-tailed deer vanished! The herd our kind have depended upon since the old times. We had nothing! Nothing . . .'

The lion slumped into silence. Rana looked up, her eyes wide.

'You don't think . . . ?'

'I think I do,' said Fenn. 'Oh dear.'

'Who have you told about this?'

Lyricon looked down at Rana and Fenn. The three were gathered in Dragon Cave, speaking in hushed voices.

'No-one yet,' said Rana. 'Is it true?'

'Is what true?' Lyricon had an anxious air.

'That you magicked the food away from the cave lions to give to us?'

Lyricon scowled. 'You were very happy with the deer!'

'But we thought you magicked them up out of nothing!'

Lyricon had his head bent low and his brow furrowed, like a cub who had just been told off for being greedy.

'Listen, my little *fliffer-hoffer*,' he said. 'Things don't really come out of nothing. I told you, it was a Finding Spell. I sort of *found* them.'

'So, you admit it!' said Fenn.

'Does *he* have to be here?' groaned Lyricon, pointing his spiky tail at Fenn.

Rana ignored this. 'What did you do?'

Lyricon pulled a face. 'Hmm. Putting it into terms that an idiot can understand,' here he looked at Fenn, 'I don't have the power to magic up white-tailed deer and so on out of thin air. But there are . . . workarounds. Look, I was afraid for my life. I knew I had to produce some results fast, so I found them from wherever I could. I didn't care who they belonged to!'

'In other words, you took all the food from the cave lions and magicked it to Howling Rock. Which started a war!'

'Yes!' exploded Lyricon. 'A war that you, personally, came very well out of, I might add!'

Rana suddenly felt very tired. The last couple of days had been big ones. 'If I tell the Seven Fangs that you took the food away from the cave lions, Sly will think that is brilliant and tell you to keep doing it.'

Lyricon smiled bitterly. 'You know him well,' he said.

'But it wouldn't be fair,' she carried on. 'Plus, if we keep doing it, the cave lions will keep coming back, hungrier and angrier, year after year, and then we will spend all our lives having wars, and not—'

'And not hunting, howling and having fun,' said Lyricon.

Rana nodded.

'I prefer not to tell the Seven Fangs about your "workyround",' Rana said.

Lyricon raised his head on its long neck and seemed to breathe more freely. A little glimmer returned to his eyes.

'You are wise, Rana,' he said. 'I chose my spokeswolf well.'

'But we can't carry on stealing food from others,' Rana replied. She rubbed her brow with a hind leg in a thoughtful manner. 'How about, from now on, we think of something really clever and crazily brilliant that works better for everyone?'

CHAPTER 17

Lyricon listened to the sounds of Howling Rock at noon. That slight whistling was Silver snoring below. Then came the short happy caws of the ravens who took advantage of the wolves' siesta to sneak in and enjoy some leftover deer. For a while, all was peaceful.

Of course, he would tell the little *fliffer-hoffer* what he was planning. Lyricon imagined the scene that would follow. 'I am going to escape,' he announced to Imaginary Rana in his head. 'And it will involve—'

Rana is a wolf, he told himself. *She will have to tell her pack if I reveal my plan to her. Her father is one of the Seven Fangs, for* plook's *sake!*

Hmm . . . of course, he would *not* tell her what he was planning.

And it was such a very dangerous plan.

He could not be blamed. Her rather tantalising tale about a magic pool that could heal his broken wing had turned out to be a dead end, apparently. And yet, he could readily believe it. There was so much magic in the air in Hunter's Reach; the crystals that lay around in the dirt here were full of memories of ancient sun, little pockets of magic power. And the wolves—yes, they were far brighter than the rather unimaginative ones back home, furry savages that certainly could not have kept *him* prisoner for a minute.

Still, if he could not fly away, there was always an alternative.

It had not seemed to occur to the *mubbimurkers* for one second the danger they were flirting with, keeping him prisoner. A dragon, in the clutches of wolves. It was an indignity his kind would punish.

He liked the idea of Sly and Silver being punished. And some of the others, the so-called guards and warriors. They still debated the best way to kill a dragon when they had nothing else to gossip about.

Did they really not care if he heard them?

He shifted his good right wing into the sunlight and felt a faint, but pleasing, tingle of magic kindling in his blood.

He would give them a last bit of magic or two before he left. But leave he certainly would.

CHAPTER 18

'A source of delicious food, grown right on our doorstep, ours forever and no jealous cave lions breathing down our manes,' said Rana.

Darkmane and Ayala regarded her thoughtfully.

'Well, what do you think?' Ayala asked, turning to her mate.

Rana's father was gnawing a deer's thigh-bone. It was breakfast time in the Starlight den. 'I think that should be enough to persuade them to free the dragon,' he said. 'His wing is still broken, after all, so he wouldn't get very far if he tried to run away.'

'But no eternal herd of bison,' said Rana. 'That's just something out of a cub-story.'

'Hmm . . . OK. It was a nice idea, though. Very well, I'll put your proposal to the other Six Fangs.'

Rana was overjoyed when she brought their reply back to Lyricon.

'The Seven Fangs have agreed. If you can deliver as promised, then they will at least let you out of the chamber and move around Hunter's Reach. As long as you promise not to breathe fire. Silver said: "He will be as free as any of the pack. Free to stay here, among us."'

Lyricon did not react at first. There seemed to be many thoughts crossing his mind as he tapped his longest claw against his chin.

'Well, it's something,' he said at last. 'It might stop me going crazy in this little cave. Can we trust them?'

'I-I think so.' She decided not to mention what Darkmane had said about the dragon not being able to run away.

'Alright,' Lyricon replied. 'I'll believe the best of them. For one last time.'

'So, little one, what are you up to now?'

Karla had appeared behind Rana, making her

jump. Rana gave the old storyteller an affectionate nuzzle. They were watching several wolves scratching at the ground around Howling Rock. There were small scrapes in the soil everywhere.

'I'm supervising,' said Rana.

'Hmm . . . congratulations. At the tender age of just over a year, you have attained the ultimate achievement of doing nothing.'

Rana grinned. 'Except my "nothing" is pretty cool,' she said. 'It is a dragon-type of nothing, until it turns into a big something.'

They watched as more wolves came to drop seeds into the ground and kick soil over them.

'Wolf-apple seeds,' explained Rana. 'Gathered by runners from all over Hunter's Reach. There's going to be some magic,' she added. 'Wait and see.'

Karla shook her head. 'Always with the magic, these days,' she said. 'I hope you know what you are doing.'

It was midnight. There was no moon, and Rana stepped out of the entrance to Howling Rock. With her ears pricked up, she lifted her snout and sniffed the air. Good—nowolf around. She didn't want any careless pups messing up this spell, or Lyricon's chance of freedom.

Padding lightly on the bare ground, she carried the hollow half-gourd by its stalk to the middle of the area the pack's efforts had prepared for the spell earlier that day. The soil was now all scratched up and kicked over. Countless seeds, gathered by the runners from the farthest corners of Hunter's Reach, lay beneath. Inside the dry shell of the gourd, a dark liquid—concocted by Lyricon—shimmered, reflecting the light from the starry sky. Rana was careful not to tilt the gourd. She could not lose a single drop.

Fenn followed her, a tiny crystal in his front teeth. Somewhere up above, Lyricon had to be peering down at them, wondering if they would remember to do exactly as he said. Rana placed the gourd down. She nodded at Fenn, who then dropped the crystal into the liquid. It vanished with a tiny but satisfying *plop*. Then they both turned tail and ran back towards the Rock as if their lives depended on it.

In moments, the two young wolves were back in Dragon Cave alongside Lyricon, gazing down at the ground. Already, a pale mist was curling up out of the gourd and beginning to spread across the land below. The mist had a faint sparkle to it, like the ice crystals that can be seen in the dawn air on the coldest winter morning.

'Now we wait,' said the dragon.

They did not have to wait long. In the morning light, the mist had melted away, revealing a change in the barren surface. All around the dawn-facing side of Howling Rock, the fresh green leaves of little wolf-apple trees could be seen, gleaming with dew. They appeared to toss their heads in the breeze as they continued to grow, reaching upwards with curling branches.

By noon, an orchard, like a great green crescent, surrounded one half of the wolves' home. Branches shimmered with purple-and-yellow blossoms. By evening, Rana and Fenn were crunching on the first apples.

'Well, we do have to test them.' Fenn grinned.

'A tiny bit underripe,' said Rana. 'They'll be perfect in an hour or so, I guess.'

And so it was that on a golden, sunny afternoon, the wolves of the Great Pack were called in by the runners to visit Home Orchard, as it was named. Happy sounds of munching filled the air, as wolves chattered and cubs played.

'Sunstreak thought up the name. It sounds good, doesn't it?' Rana said to Karla.

'Is Home Orchard a good name?' Karla frowned. 'Wolves shouldn't really have a home. I mean, the whole world should be our home, not one little bit of it.'

'Oh, you don't like anything!' protested Rana.

'I like *you*,' said Karla. 'And I like wolf apples. But I'm not sure about all these dragonish ideas!'

'This isn't a dragonish idea,' said Rana. 'It was *my* idea, and Fenn's. Lyricon just used his magic to make it happen.'

'Food should be found not grown,' grumbled Karla. 'It will never catch on.'

Just then, Rana noticed Fenn was hovering on the edge of the new orchard, frowning and not going in.

'Go on, enjoy!' she urged. 'You helped grow it!'

Fenn eyed the leafy ways of the orchard, bushy with fast-grown undergrowth.

'I don't know,' he said. 'Something isn't right. I—' His nose began to twitch.

'Really?' Rana groaned. 'Your special Scent again?'

'Well . . .'

There was a sudden yelp from Scruff, one of the youngest cubs, as he sprang out of the trees. Then two more cubs came rushing out, wild-eyed.

Rana looked puzzled. 'Now what?'

Next came Riki, leaping and looking behind him as if he was being pursued. A couple of the older wolves came trotting over to investigate.

'Some game or other?' said Darkmane, as Riki fled past him.

'Monster!' cried Riki.

Rana joined her father, curious. They were just about to enter under the boughs when another couple of howls erupted from within the trees and several more wolves raced out.

'Come on,' growled a voice. 'Something's up.'

It was Sly, coming to see what the fuss was about. 'You're coming too!' he said to Rana. 'It's your orchard!'

The chiefs began to creep under the leaves, with Rana following. Something was crashing towards them through the bushy growth ahead, a dark bulk in the shadows.

Sly and Darkmane exchanged looks.

'W-what is that?' gasped Sly. The wolves backed away. Suddenly, it emerged from the leaves. Rana's eyes almost popped out.

'A ladybird!' said Rana. 'Except it's the size of a warthog!'

The wolves just stared as the giant shiny bug waddled out. Its wing-covers were rosy red and mottled with pretty black spots. As they watched, the enormous bug stopped in the sun for a while, then opened the gleaming casing of its back, unfurled a vast pair of gossamer wings and took off.

This startled Sly and Darkmane, who jumped about briefly before resuming their calm exteriors with a faint air of embarrassment.

Fenn gave a slight giggle. They all watched the great bug disappear over the nearest ridge and off towards the mountains.

'Well?' Sly stared at Rana.

Lyricon laughed aloud when he heard about the ladybird. Rana was even forced to tell the story again, omitting no detail.

'And Sly jumped out of his fur as it took off! Oh dear, if only I had been there.'

'There is a serious side to this too,' said Rana. 'I mean, why—'

'Well, it's obvious,' Lyricon said airily. 'It seems my growing spell has also affected insects in the area. The orchard must be scoured for any more surprises.'

In no time at all, Rana had reported back to the Seven Fangs.

'Sort this out yourself,' said Sly. 'Get the warriors to help you.'

Everywolf waited while the warriors entered the orchard in teams to hunt for giant insects. A sun spider the size of a small goat chased two of the warriors straight back out before Temper, Stalker pack's top warrior, pounced on it and flattened it. A great cheer went up.

Darkmane's team was the first to finish their work, and he emerged crunching on a giant grasshopper with a contented look.

'Greedy!' shouted out Fenn.

Right at the end of the operation, all the watching cubs gave an 'ooh' of delight when a golden woolly bear moth flitted up from the middle of the trees and flew away.

Rana smiled. 'The reign of the monster insects is over,' she said. General feeding soon began again, although most wolves stayed around the edges of the orchard.

'We were lucky,' said Fenn, as they looked down from Lyricon's cave later. 'Suppose there had been a giant assassin bug in there, or a humungous black widow spider. I would have had to go in and rescue the little cubs!'

'Well, it was a mistake.' Rana sighed. 'But yes, we could have been looking at dead wolves coming out of that place, not pretty moths.'

Rana looked at Lyricon, who was sitting staring into space. Finding new patterns for the crystals didn't seem to interest him that much, at the moment.

'Is there always a drawback with magic?' she asked.

'Oh yes,' he replied. 'You must never forget that.'

CHAPTER 19

Soon, the giant insects were just a memory, a funny tale, if anything, to amuse the cubs. On the long sunny days, the orchard now became the place to be. Cubs played there, families fed there, everywolf snoozed there.

'Howling Rock has changed completely,' Rana said to Lyricon. 'Now it's a place of greenery, a sort of paradise. That's how I used to picture it when I was a cub and Karla told me tales about it. It's a dream you've made come true.'

'All on his own,' muttered Fenn.

'Oh yes, even little what's-his-name helped a bit, I suppose,' said Lyricon. He kept peering down at the activity below. 'I must say I'm quite astonished at you wolves and your appetite for fruit. I thought you only ate deer and bison and so on.'

'Ah well, there is a story about that,' said Rana. 'They say that, in the Far-off Times, Fera and her wolves grew so successful as a pack, they hunted the other animals to the brink of extinction.'

'I can believe it,' said Lyricon. 'You are a greedy lot.'

'Exactly!' said Rana. 'The Sun warned Fera not to be greedy, but she would not listen. A day came when the wolves could find no more animals to hunt. Fera became very hungry. But more than that, she became very sad. She missed the great bison bellowing, the young deer skipping, the hares boxing in the fields. She did something she had never done before—she lay down and cried.

'The Sun looked down and took pity. From the place where Fera's tears had fallen, a tree grew. In no time, green fruit appeared on it. The sun helped the tree to grow, and others like it. The wolves tasted the green fruit and liked them, calling them wolf apples. Because of wolf apples, the wolves stopped hunting prey so greedily, and the deer and other animals gradually returned.'

'And they all live happily ever after, I suppose?'

'Of course.' Rana smiled. 'So now, whenever prey becomes scarce, wolves will always turn to fruit for their food.'

'A cautionary tale,' said Lyricon. 'I just hope the council are fond enough of wolf apples to think I deserve a proper reward.'

At that he fell silent, his scaly tail twitching as he peered out of the crack in the cave wall at the shimmering green leaves below.

He needs his freedom now, thought Rana. *But will they give it to him?*

Later that day, the Seven Fangs visited Dragon Cave.

'We are most delighted with you,' Silver said. 'I'm so pleased I had the vision to insist you not be slain.'

Lyricon made a bow. Only Rana realised it was rather a mocking one.

'I am here but to please,' he said. 'Seeing your people crunching wolf apples and frolicking in the sun has touched my heart. Now, if I can perhaps touch yours . . . ?'

'You seek your reward?' said Sly. 'By all means. We will fetch you as much fish as you like.'

'I already have the fish I need,' the dragon said coldly. 'Rana sees to that.'

Silver frowned. 'Perhaps some entertainment? I could tell you stories of my family history. My great-uncle Copperknot had some most interesting diseases.'

Rana thought Lyricon was going to explode.

'Not *those* kinds of rewards!' she cried out. 'You promised Lyricon his freedom for a reliable supply of food.'

'Uh-uh,' countered Sly. 'We promised we would consider it. And we are always considering it.'

'We continue to consider it,' said Silver. 'But the time is not yet right.'

'Come now,' growled Darkmane. 'I was there, and you promised—'

'The echoes can be very bad in the Chamber of the Seven Fangs,' said Silver, with a slightly mocking tone. 'People hear what they want to hear.'

'Indeed,' agreed Sly. He turned to the rest of the chiefs.

Haze and Chiggers grunted in agreement. Finally, Hunter of Lightning pack nodded too. Only Sunstreak and Darkmane stood against them.

'Whatever we said then—or did not say—you are certainly outvoted now,' said Sly.

A silence fell upon the chamber.

It was broken by Rana. 'Lyricon is too proud to beg for himself, so I will. He needs freedom, to be out in the sun, to see the forest, smell the air! No creature should be shut up like this, day after day!'

The council seemed taken aback by her emotion. Rana searched their faces for a hopeful sign.

'We are the children of Fera,' she said with passion. 'Freedom is in our blood! How can we deny it to a friend like Lyricon?'

There was a brief pause, then Sly spoke up.

'Very easily,' he said. 'We need him here, doing his magic—not running round the forest, smelling air, breathing fire or planning his getaway.'

'I agree,' said Silver. 'And with his wing still broken, he might get killed by a bear or kidnapped by the cave lions or something. He's safest here. And we're safest with him here.'

Rana looked at Darkmane, but he gave a tiny shake of his head; he could only back her so far.

'I'm sorry,' he said gently. 'We must run with the pack and do what is best for all.'

‘We will bring you treats, as I said,’ added Sly. ‘And you will be grateful for it.’

That evening, the fresh salmon had a bitter taste for Lyricon. He barely touched it, and chewed the end of his tail instead, like a sulky cub. Rana noticed that he showed no interest in moving his crystals around either. Fenn had wandered off, bored, and the pair were alone.

‘I’m sorry about the Seven Fangs,’ she said, hanging her head. ‘I really thought they would keep their promise. I was stupid.’

Lyricon looked bleak. ‘When you talked about freedom being in your blood, I thought you were going to inspire them. I could almost taste the freedom!’

He peered out through a crack at the pine forest in the distance. Rays from the setting sun broke through the clouds and seemed to dance across it, forever out of reach.

‘We were both fools to believe them,’ he said.

Rana had been deep in thought. ‘I’ll tell you what,’ she said. ‘I’m a storyteller. I could tell you tales of the forest. If you close your eyes, it’ll be just like being there. Getting lost in stories is a kind of freedom.'

Lyricon gave her an empty, dejected look. 'To another wolf, perhaps. They already know how the forest looks and sounds and smells, so they can re-create it in their mind. But I grew up on the other side of the sea, in a land of volcanoes, stone and sand.' He slumped to the floor. 'Stuck here, I can never really share your wolfish world, because I'm a dragon . . . and a prisoner.'

Rana looked at the half-blocked door of the chamber. 'If only you *were* a wolf! You'd get out of here easily.'

She settled down with a sigh. She had been trying to sleep at night, like Lyricon did, so they could be a bit more in sync. But to her surprise, he showed no sign of sleeping. Instead, he began to fumble around in his piles of unused crystals, turning them over and muttering to himself.

'Ammolite . . . there was an ammolite, I'm sure!'

Rana came to see what he was doing. 'What are you looking for?'

'We call it the Changing Stone . . .'

'What colour is it?'

'That's just it, it's many colours. Like the eye of a

dragon!' Suddenly, he snatched up a dark shard from among a pile of opals. 'This is it,' he said in a whisper.

At first, Rana could see nothing special in the stone, but as Lyricon held it in his claws, tilting it to the moonlight, it flashed with facets of deep blood red and the richest pond-slime green.

'It's a good one,' he said, breathing on it, then rubbing it against the soft skin of one of the folds of his wings.

Rana became caught up in his excitement. 'What can it do?'

'Tales of the old sorcerers, the Crystalists, have been coming back to me,' he said. 'If I remember correctly, this stone can help me transform—but only for a little while, and only if I have something to copy . . .'

Lyricon gazed intently at Rana; he seemed to be thinking furiously. 'Yes—yes, I can do it.'

'Do what? Why are you looking at me like that?' she asked, frowning.

Lyricon made an effort to calm down. 'You want me to share your world?'

'Of course.'

'And you agree that I have earned a respite from

being stuck in here?'

'You know I do!'

'So, here's the plan. I turn myself into a copy of you.'

CHAPTER 20

'I can only stay a wolf for a few hours,' Lyricon explained. 'I must return here to the Changing Stone by sunrise. If I fail to do so . . . I will be stuck in wolf form forever.'

Rana gazed at him, wide-eyed. 'Wow. Is—is it worth the risk?'

Lyricon nodded. 'I need to get out of here—just for a while. Otherwise, I'll go crazy.'

For a moment, they just stared at each other.

'OK. Let's do it.'

Rana had never seen Lyricon quite so focused as they built the crystal spiral together, making sure everything was in place. As he positioned the ammolite in the centre of the pattern, the stone seemed to come alive—glistening emerald and scarlet, shifting constantly between the two.

Rana's body tingled, as a soft glow surrounded them both. Then it was over. No explosion or shower of stars, just Rana face to face with . . . herself.

'Whoa.'

Rana, of course, had seen magic before, but this fazed her. 'Fera's fangs! You look just like me.'

'Duh. That *is* the whole point of the spell. I'm a sort of echo of you, if you like.'

'Then that's what we'll call you: Echo,' said Rana. 'If any guard sees you, I'll say you're a long-lost cousin or something.' She paused. 'Er . . . what are you doing?'

'Echo' was twitching his nose in a peculiar way. 'Scenting!' he said. 'Now I'm a wolf, I have this amazing nose! It's incredible. I can smell the orchard leaves outside, and rain on the night air! And—phew—I can also smell the dozens of stinky wolves that I share this rock with.'

'You'll learn to like it.' Rana grinned.

Now Lyricon was practically bouncing around the room, leaping like a playful cub.

'I'm so light!' he said. 'No flab on you wolves—you're all muscle and fur.' He stopped and calmed down, his tongue hanging out as he panted. 'Feels weird.'

'What happened to your broken wing?' asked Rana.

'As a wolf, I don't have it,' he replied. 'But I do have a nasty ache above my left front leg. That is probably my body remembering it.'

'Well, you look pretty mobile,' Rana said. 'Come on, you can do your springing around outside Howling Rock. But keep in the shadows and try not to be noticed. Darkmane will *not* believe you're my long-lost cousin! Neither will Fenn.'

They were in luck. Only Boulder was on guard at the main way out, and he was having a nap.

'I love the security in this place,' joked Echo.

'Shush,' hissed Rana. 'We're not in the clear yet.' She plunged straight into the shadows of the wolf-apple orchard, Echo on her heels.

'It's weird being small,' he whispered, as they crept to the far edge. 'All the trees look enormous.'

There was a short dash from under the boughs of Home Orchard to the pines of Frost Forest.

'Stay low,' Rana ordered, as Gripper and another warrior wolf trotted in the distance, on patrol.

'There, you see?' she said. 'Security. Now run!'

The pair were soon in the deep tracks of the great forest. Rana took Echo to see the crater by the Rushing Waters. It had turned into a pond with some curious little frogs peeping out. The trees and grass were starting to grow back, but the land was still scorched far and wide.

'This is where you crash-landed,' said Rana.

'Wow,' said Echo. 'Look at the site! I was lucky to survive this.'

'So was I!' Rana laughed, stroking her tattered mane with a front paw.

'You are never going to let me forget that,' said Echo.

She watched quietly as he padded around the crater, sniffing and scratching at the earth like a cub.

'It's amazing,' said Echo. 'As a dragon, I'm used to flying over the scenery. I mean, frankly, I'm pretty blasé about it. But seeing it with a wolf's eyes, and hearing everything with a wolf's ears . . . it's beautiful. I feel like I'm twice as alive as I usually am.'

'Really?' Rana loved hearing Lyricon saying nice things about being a wolf.

'I'm better at seeing things move, too,' he said. 'Look over there. I'm getting a strange urge to hunt those rabbits.'

Rana followed his gaze to see several rabbits grazing on a slope. 'Cottontails,' she said. 'Copy me. I'll show you how we hunt.' Instead of making straight for the rabbits, she took a cautious route behind some scrub.

'Rabbits are quite fast and can be hard to chase,' said Rana. 'Lie down here, by this bush, and we'll let them come to us. Then we can ambush them.'

'How do you know they'll come this way?'

'They might not,' whispered Rana. 'So, then we'll slowly move in on them. When they're close, we'll suddenly give chase.'

They crouched low behind the scrub, peering through the thorns and leaves to see what the rabbits would do.

'You wolves really are part of the land, aren't you?' observed Echo. 'You see everything at the same level as your prey. You feel the grass beneath your feet, the wet leaves against your face, smell the soil.'

'Of course,' said Rana. 'Everything affects the hunt. A rabbit will run and leap differently on soft ground, for example.'

'It's different for dragons,' said Echo. 'We don't need to creep up on things or track them carefully. We hunt from the sky, looking down at our prey. When we spot them, we just swoop down.'

'But you can't see through trees or leaves,' said Rana. 'It must be easy for prey to escape.'

'It is at night,' Echo said. 'Dragons don't see that well in the dark. But we do alright by daylight. Dragons that prefer meat eat a lot of it. So back home, we only bother to hunt large herds of bison or deer, animals you can spot from miles away . . . and are rubbish at hiding.'

Rana pondered this. If she was ever hunted by a dragon, she reckoned she would manage to escape. *They can fly and do magic*, she thought, *but on the ground, we are more elusive—trickier.*

'Hush, here they come.' Four cottontails were hopping slowly towards the scrub where the wolves were waiting. Suddenly, a dark shape dropped from the sky, and in a blur of motion, snatched the smallest rabbit and soared upwards. The other three cottontails scattered into the underbrush.

'There goes the demonstration!' Rana grinned. 'The owl got there first.'

'Nice hunting,' said Echo. 'Dragon style.'

Staring at the rising moon behind the ridge of trees at Pine Top, Rana spotted something else.

'There's Karla,' she said. 'I wonder what she's doing out this way? Let's take a peek.'

The pair trotted along a narrow deer track to the foot of a rocky trail. As they made their way up the ridge, they could hear Karla talking in a low voice.

'Who's she speaking to?' wondered Rana. She and Echo watched from a distance as Karla sat silhouetted against the starry sky.

'Looks like she's talking to the rocks,' said Echo.

Rana stared at the big, bulky shadow next to Karla. 'That's not a rock,' she said quietly. 'That's Greyface.'

Karla was actually holding a conversation with the Old Man of the Woods, the great grizzly it had taken two packs to drive away from the elk carcass.

The old storyteller did not seem afraid at all. It was a most peculiar sight to see a wolf and a bear grunting and barking quietly together. Occasionally, Greyface would let out some gruff roar that made Rana jump.

The most peculiar thing was that, listening closely, Rana began to feel she could understand some of what Greyface was saying. If you ignored the growls and harsh tones of speech, many of the words were like the ones wolves used.

'That bear is terrifying!' whispered Echo. 'When you're wolf-sized!'

'Shush,' said Rana. 'I think he's leaving. Stay in the shadows.'

Greyface began to lumber off down the ridge, surprisingly quiet for his vast size as he melted into the night. Karla sat for a long time, peering after him.

Then she spoke again. 'You can come out now, little one.'

Rana couldn't help but smile. Of course, a wily old wolf like Karla would not be spied on easily.

'Still with the "little one"?' said Rana, as she sprang up onto the rock next to Karla. The old wolf gave her an affectionate nuzzle.

'You will always be a little one to me,' said Karla. 'I have known your scent and your tread ever since you were the tiniest cub.' She flicked an ear with a hindpaw. 'I imagine you are most astonished at what you have just seen.'

'Well, yes,' said Rana. 'You did tell me you spoke to birds, but I never imagined—'

'Birds, beavers, bears—in the Far-off Times, the Sun gave all creatures the same language,' Karla said. 'The First Tongue is still there underneath the shrill of the hawk and the grunt of the bear. It sometimes takes a bit of flattery and extremely good manners to start up a conversation, but it is always worth it. Sadly, today it is just not done to speak to other creatures. Wolves have grown suspicious and mostly keep to themselves.'

'Dad always said—'

'Darkmane is far too set in his ways. You have a livelier mind, Rana. I can hear it in everything you say. And although you are a storyteller, you also have a responsibility to listen. Bears have knowledge that wolves cannot dream of. They live twice as long as we do, you know.'

'And sleep half of it,' said Rana, with a smile.

Karla went silent for a moment, a cloud passing over her brow.

'Greyface shared news,' she said. 'There's been some talk among the seabirds—the ones that fly the farthest over the ocean. A gull heard from a shearwater that some great dark flying things, too big to be birds, have been seen from time to time, out over the Barren Isles. They went back and forth, as if searching for something.'

A dread chill shivered down Rana's spine. To her, this could only mean one thing.

'Er . . . the Barren Isles are a long way away, aren't they?' she asked.

'A very long way away,' said Karla. 'But I must still warn the Seven Fangs.'

Rana scratched at an ear. 'Will they trust news from a bear?'

Karla huffed. 'Sly will laugh at me, and Silver will probably accuse me of trying to stir up dragon trouble. But a storyteller has a duty to tell the truth, welcome or not. And maybe the others will listen. Will you join me on the run home?'

Rana wanted to, but she was conscious of Echo close by—probably wondering what was taking so long. She shook her head, eyes bright. 'I've got dragon business of my own. You go ahead!'

And she was off before Karla could say another word.

CHAPTER 21

'You took your time!' Echo said when Rana returned to his hiding place. 'Remember I have to be back in the cave by dawn, or you will be stuck with a twin forever,' Echo said. 'And I'm sure I could be a very annoying sibling. Just saying.'

Rana ignored this. 'Did you hear what Greyface said to Karla?' she asked. 'Rumours of enormous, winged creatures flying over the distant islands. What do you think? Could it be your kind, looking for you?'

'I doubt it,' said Lyricon. 'It's been so long—they probably think I'm dead.'

He looked thoughtful. It was weird for Rana to

see her own face—yet not her face—frowning back at her.

'Even if by chance—a miraculous chance—they flew right overhead, how would they spot me? After tonight, I am going to be stuck in Howling Rock again. They wouldn't have a hope of seeing me. No dragon, certainly not the proud race I come from, would ever expect another dragon to be the prisoner of wolves.'

For a moment, Echo looked so downcast that Rana was filled with pity. She was about to suggest another rabbit hunt to cheer him up when they were interrupted by a gentle trilling of high-pitched notes.

'It's the lark,' Rana cried out.

'So? Is that another one of your favourite singers?' teased Echo.

'You don't get it,' she replied. 'We wolves have a saying: "When the lark it sings, the dawn it brings." Sunrise is maybe an hour away. We have to hurry!'

Rana glanced through the treetops to see mist rising from Deadwolf Creek below. They were much further from home than she would like to be, with sun-up approaching. Taking a gamble, she rushed Echo through a brambly gorge (without too many complaints), then scrambled down a steep ridge in search of one of the pack's regular tracks back home.

The moment they started down the track they heard fast-moving feet thrashing along the trail ahead of them, getting closer. Suddenly, Lightfoot appeared.

'Rana, what are you doing all the way out here?'

Echo had leapt to hide—unsuccessfully—behind a bush. Lightfoot blinked at him, puzzled. 'And who's this?'

'Er . . . Echo from Horizon pack. He, um . . . doesn't get out much. We had an urgent errand for the dragon. Um, what's the quickest way home?'

With Lightfoot's advice, the pair raced for Howling Rock as fast as their legs could go.

Boulder was never quite sure what happened that night, when just before sunrise, two wolves that looked like Rana raced past him into Howling Rock. Maybe he had seen double. Or maybe he had fallen asleep and was dreaming. Nevertheless, the pair made it back into Dragon Cave just as the sun's first rays were beginning to creep through the highest cracks in the walls.

With relief, Echo touched the ammolite stone. He waited. Nothing happened. The two wolves exchanged a look of panic. Echo touched the stone again, this time with both paws. There was a loud crack and the gem shattered, exploding with a bright flash. Rana's eyes were dazzled for a moment. She blinked and then saw Lyricon—the dragon—standing before her.

'We did it!' she said.

Lyricon stared gloomily at the broken crystal.

'We're back, you're safe!' Rana repeated, nudging him with her snout. 'You're a dragon again. We got away with it.'

'Yes, but we pushed our luck by arriving at the last moment,' Lyricon sighed. 'The ammolite is destroyed. Now I'm trapped again.'

Rana joined him to gaze in a forlorn fashion at the smoking bits of shattered crystal.

'We'd better get some rest,' she said. Then added awkwardly, 'Um, I might have to talk to Karla later, so I could be away with my pack for a day or so. Will you be alright?'

Lyricon appeared to be lost in thought. But then, as she started to squeeze through the rocks blocking the entrance, she heard him call her name.

'Rana?'

She turned.

'Thank you for tonight. I know you took a risk too, helping me go free without telling the pack. You're a good friend.'

Rana gave a smile and trotted away down the passage. She should have been pleased, but instead she had a strange feeling of loss, like a magical moment had gone forever.

CHAPTER 22

Lyricon stared into the darkness as Rana's pawsteps faded away. He felt overcome by a huge sadness.

It had backfired. His hours of freedom had not really made him happier. In fact, by bringing intense happiness then dashing it away, he was now plunged into an abyss of gloom.

What a beautiful world it was out there. How incredible to feel alive again, to run, to leap, to play in the moonlight. How wonderful to share it with a friend, and what's more, to see it all through the eyes of a wolf.

How vivid their senses were! Every breath had been magical. Every scent had told a story.

Wolves had shorter lives than dragons—perhaps that explained the intensity of their feelings.

He pondered as the sun rose across the sky. He could delay no longer. With Rana away for a day or two, he had time to begin his plan. He would have to leave her out of it, of course. She wouldn't like that. It was not going to be easy. And he truly hoped that one day she would understand.

CHAPTER 23

'So, you're to thank for all these treats?'

After her morning nap, Rana had bumped into Ela enjoying wolf apples for breakfast at Home Orchard. Ela looked immaculate as ever, her snowy mane in an attractive wave and her front paws crossed nonchalantly as she sat in the sunlight. 'I hear you are quite the wizard these days, making all the magic happen.'

'Ha ha,' said Rana. 'Fenn and I just help Lyricon. We don't actually do any magic.'

'I'm sure you don't,' said Ela. 'But you know how people exaggerate. I was just wondering . . .'

'Yes?'

'If you have a day off today, can I go and help at Howling Rock in your place? I'm sure there must be so much to do. All those guards to boss around.'

'I'm sure they will be very pleased to see you,' said Rana. 'Someone in the Seven Fangs will find you something to do—but don't expect to do much bossing.'

Ela gave a quick smile and raced off. 'I'll tell them you sent me,' she said.

'You are becoming quite the influential wolf if Ela is starting to drop your name!' said a voice behind her. It was Karla, padding through the trees. The old wolf gave Rana an affectionate nuzzle. 'I'm glad we could meet before I go away. I'm being sent off to do some storytelling at Spook Bay, on the north border, where Horizon scouts patrol. And then I have to invite them back to Howling Rock for Victory Day.'

'What's that?'

'Haven't you heard? Last night, Haze and Temper went to spy on the cave lions. The beasts are in disarray. Haze ran into an old lion, called Scrapper, who had been thrown out of the pack for disagreeing with Gragh. Scrapper said several of their best warriors were lost in the swamp when they fled after the battle at Thorny Gap. A big row erupted as to whether to return home to the mountains or stay in the wilderness beyond Storm Falls. Now, they are fighting among themselves—some staying by the Falls and others in the grasslands. Basically, they are beaten and demoralised, ripe for conquest, in fact. Our pack chiefs are delighted with this state of affairs. They want to celebrate this news—and all recent achievements—with a big Victory Day celebration at the next full moon.'

Rana's tail drooped. 'Well, I feel sorry for the cave lions.'

'Very sensible. Only by seeing through the eyes of all creatures can we be worthy of our place in the forest.'

'Even dragons?' Rana asked, quietly.

'We can certainly feel sorry for a lost, trapped dragon,' Karla replied. 'Without forgetting it could bring danger in its wake, like the first storm crow before a hurricane.'

A silence fell between them and Rana noticed that Karla looked sad.

'Is everything OK?' Rana asked. 'Are you worried about being sent to the North Border? It's a long lope.'

'Don't worry, Darkmane is coming with me. And I know you are old enough and wise enough to look after things here,' she added with a smile.

'Now you're making fun.'

'Well, only a little,' said the old she-wolf. 'In fact, I am seeing growing signs of wisdom in you, little one. You are more than ready for your next lesson. Meet me at sundown at the start of Cottonwood Trail. Bring a dead lizard, or a mouse or two.'

And with that intriguing invitation, Karla was gone.

Rana had the rest of the afternoon to spend with her family. She got Fenn to help her with her little hunting challenge. Catching prey was something she'd never had to do at Howling Rock, but Fenn was more than happy to join in a small-prey competition. In the end, Fenn caught two mice—one of which he ate himself—and Rana caught a lizard that had dozed too long on a sunny rock.

'What do you think about our big green friend?' asked Fenn, as they rested in the long grass. 'Is he OK?'

'Not really,' Rana said, remembering her secret adventure with 'Echo'. 'I think he's getting more desperate. That last let-down by the pack chiefs hit him hard. He'll do practically anything to escape now.'

Fenn went quiet for a while.

'I agree,' he said at last. 'And I do try my best *never* to agree with you, as you know.' He grinned. 'I think he's got some sort of plan. After all, with his magic, surely he could find a way to escape if he wanted to? I know I could, if I had that kind of power!'

Rana stopped chewing. 'So, what's he up to?'

'I don't know, but lately when he's playing with those crystals of his, the Scent starts to tickle my nose.'

'I was waiting for you to drag your Scent into it!'

'Mock me if you want, dear sister! I'm keeping an eye on him,' Fenn said. 'The Scent never lies . . .'

Twilight deepened in the darkling glades as Rana went alone to the rendezvous with Karla. She noticed that the older wolf was always looking upwards as they made their way through the pines.

'My friend likes a tall tree by a clearing, with a great view . . .' she said. It didn't take them long to spot the creature they were looking for. Perched on a half-broken branch was a substantial bird with two spiky tufts of feathers sprouting from its head, a great horned owl.

Karla dropped the offerings of prey on the edge of the clearing. She then lowered her head and tail and sat quietly at the foot of the tree. The huge bird flapped its heavy wings and dropped gracefully down to inspect the food. He seemed to accept the offering approvingly, and bent to his feast.

'Meet Huboo,' said the old she-wolf. 'You speak to him, Rana.'

Rana's heart beat fast. She was imagining what the *mubbimurkers* would say. *Keep to your own kind*, probably. Imagining the frowns of the pack chiefs made her even keener not to let Karla down.

'Hello, Huboo,' she said, in her gentlest tone.

'Hoo hoo—who are you?' hooted the owl.

'I am Rana. Daughter of Ayala and Darkmane, wolf of the Starlight pack and—'

'Not too much too fast,' whispered Karla. 'Most birds don't understand long sentences or complicated ideas. They like to say the same little things over and over again. They are like cubs, in a way.'

Rana began again. 'I'm Rana. I'm a wolf.'

‘I know that!’ hooted Huboo. ‘Do I look like a fool? Hoo hoo!’

‘He’s laughing,’ said Karla. ‘You’re off to a good start.’

They spoke about the little things, the weather, their families, and what they liked to eat. After a while, Karla took over the conversation. Then she indicated they should leave.

‘Job done,’ she said. ‘Huboo will spread the word among the other birds that you are a kind and helpful creature who should be told any important news of the forest.’

Rana headed back to her pack with a feeling of being more a part of the forest than ever. As she trotted along the moonlit trail, her joy was spoilt by a pang of pity for Lyricon, who was now cut off from the forest, and from his own kind too. How unhappy was he really—deep down? She resolved to work even harder to help him. She would not give up until he was free.

CHAPTER 24

It was with a rapid tread that Rana left the Starlight den at the foot of Howling Rock and headed for Dragon Cave.

It had been lovely to spend time with her mother and all the little cubs she knew so well. Now however, a new day was beginning, and the task of helping her friend was all that mattered.

As she loped up to the entrance, she stopped in her tracks. Merry laughter from inside greeted her ears. She recognised the cackle of Lyricon, and a sort of light, yappy titter. Rana hurried to the top chamber and was surprised to find Ela crouched before Lyricon.

'Hi, Ranny,' Ela said, looking round. 'We've been having such a laugh!'

'Y-you have?'

'Yes,' Lyricon beamed. 'Run along, Ela, and I'll tell Rana all about it. Go and check on our special project.'

Ela trotted out, looking pleased with herself. Left alone, Rana looked up at Lyricon with a searching gaze.

'Well, this is a big change,' she began. 'When I left, you were all sad about being trapped again.'

'Exactly,' said Lyricon. 'I realised I had to pick myself up and find another way forward. My experience as Echo made me feel more like part of the pack. So now, it's time for me, Lyricon, to be accepted as one of you. If I get to know everywolf, then they will get to know me—and finally trust me, I hope.'

Rana tried to hide her scepticism. 'I suppose it—it might work,' she said.

'And there's no need for you to be always running around as my servant,' he added. 'I made some, er . . . non-magical plans yesterday and Ela is keen to help. Just look at what we've been doing in your absence.'

Lyricon held up a long, colourful rod. It was almost as long as a full-grown wolf and made of many gems.

Rana stared blankly at the rather garish, sparkly object. She felt a slight tingle creep through her mane.

'What is it?'

'It is part of a work of art,' said Lyricon. 'Ela told me all about Victory Day, and it gave me an idea. I can prove my loyalty to the Great Pack by presenting a beautiful gift to the Seven Fangs for the celebration. One that doesn't use any magic at all.'

Rana frowned. 'It feels magical to me.'

'Oh, it's bound to,' Lyricon replied airly. 'I'm using a lot of the crystals we've used once before. They still have some *fiffle-zakkle*—I mean, latent magical energy—but are no good for any proper spells.'

Rana continued to eye the object doubtfully. The phrase 'latent magical energy' meant about as much to her as *fiffle-zakkle* did.

'And this sparkly stick is your . . . art?' she asked.

'Yes,' enthused Lyricon. 'It's part of a Victory Tower, a monument to celebrate all our triumphs. The finished piece will go right on top of Howling Rock and be unveiled on the big day.'

Rana looked at the shiny piece of 'art' and tried to

like it, but it seemed rather ugly and pointless. Also, she felt left out. She was usually right at the centre of all Lyricon's schemes.

Just then, Fenn appeared in the chamber. 'What have I missed?' he asked. 'I hear Ela is working here now.'

'And doing great things,' said Lyricon. 'Go up and take a look.'

Rana nudged Fenn back out the door. They climbed up the honeycomb of caves out onto the top of the Rock. It was windy and bright. Rana tried not to look down at the great drop to the canyon below. Peering ahead, she saw the monument being constructed. Most of it was lying on the rocks, getting fussed over by wolves. The sun was behind the clouds, and frankly, the great work of art did not look very impressive.

She sighed. 'Oh well, if it makes him happy.'

'Bad, bad, bad.'

Rana looked round. A magpie nearby had started to squawk and chirrup in an insistent fashion. But to Rana's ears, it was bringing a message. Another magpie landed right next to the artwork.

'Bad thing, bad thing . . .'

'Can you hear that?' she asked Fenn.

'A lot of noisy magpies, not much else,' he replied.

'Bad, bad!' they called again. Now, both birds were standing by the shiny tower that lay across the top of the Rock.

Are they trying to get my attention? Rana moved closer to the unfinished artwork and had another look. In fact, she took a very long look. Because as she stared, she realised she had seen that tower before.

'Fenn—it's the one I told you about!' Rana whispered. 'The secret magic Lyricon was working on.'

'What are you talking about?'

'This artwork of his! I didn't realise at first. But if you picture it standing up, it looks just like a bigger version of the tower I saw him making a couple of weeks ago. You know, that night he said he needed a rest—then didn't take one.'

'So what? Does it matter?'

'I think so. I'm sure the magpies think it matters too. Maybe they can sense something. And not just dragon *fiffle-zakkle* either!'

Rana and Fenn gazed at the sculpture on the ground. It was connected to a system of vines, all ready to be hauled up into place when it was finished. The completed tower would flash like fire on top of Howling Rock. Fenn wrinkled his nose and his eyes widened.

'You too?'

'Yes. It's definitely setting off the Scent.'

The pair gazed at the artwork in silence. Ela was trotting back and forth, giving orders here and there. With a last unhappy cry, the magpies flew away.

Fenn looked worried. 'Remember I told you that I thought Lyricon had some sort of plan? Well, this could be it.'

'Is everything OK?' asked Lyricon. 'You seem a little distracted.'

Rana had returned to the Dragon Cave and was sorting glittery stones from the others with a troubled look on her face.

'Are you not impressed by the Victory Tower? Are you worried that I will become an artist and give up being a sorcerer?' He said this with a teasing smile, but she did not respond.

There was a silence. For once, Fenn also said nothing. Lyricon shifted his wings in a dragonish shrug and went back to work, trying to fashion some gold nuggets into a flower shape.

Rana chose her next words carefully. 'Why did you say the tower was an idea that you only just had after hearing about Victory Day?'

Lyricon continued to work on his gold flower. 'Because it was.'

'But—' Rana was anxious about voicing her doubts. In the end, she couldn't help herself. 'You had this idea weeks ago.'

There followed an uncomfortable pause.

'Why do you, um . . . say that?' the dragon asked.

'I—I came back here one night when you said you needed to rest. I'd collected more rankweed to help you feel better. But you weren't sleeping. You were making a miniature version of your tower.'

Lyricon turned his head towards Rana. His eyes seemed to burn into her.

'And did you see what it could do?'

Rana looked at the floor. 'Some kind of magic,' she said quietly. 'And you said this wasn't really magic.'

Lyricon sat in thought, lowering his eyelids. His tail swished behind him distractedly.

'And are there any other times when you have

been spying on me?' he asked. The atmosphere in the room seemed to darken.

'Not spying!' protested Rana. 'I've never been spying! I just don't understand why you're keeping secrets.'

'That's just it!' cried Lyricon. 'The magic part is *supposed* to be a secret, a surprise for you all.'

Silence fell between the two. At last, Lyricon spoke. 'I don't like the feeling that you don't trust me.' His voice had turned cold.

'I did trust you until you started all this *fiffle-zakkle*,' she snapped back.

'Well, I can't work with someone who doesn't trust me,' he said. Then slowly, deliberately, he gathered his jewels to him and turned his back to her. 'Please leave.'

Rana blinked. She could not believe this. After all she had done for him. After all they had shared.

In a fury, she walked out.

CHAPTER 25

A few days later, Rana had still not returned to Dragon Cave. Only Fenn shared her suspicions, and he agreed they could do nothing but watch and wait until the tower was completed. Nowolf else knew enough about dragon magic to understand. Sly and Silver would certainly not listen to their vague unease about Lyricon's new 'artwork'.

In the meantime, Rana took over Karla's job telling stories to the cubs during the day, and practised patrolling with scouts and other yearlings in the evening.

For a while, absorbed in finally finding her place in the Great Pack, all the complications of her recent life—dragons, golems, cave lions and crystals—melted away.

It seemed that Ela was Lyricon's chief helper now. And Rana saved her anger about that for the hunt. She stalked the meandering trails around Howling Rock, daring a deer, an elk, or even a bear to cross her path.

She was returning home one evening when Lightfoot called out to her.

'Here you are at last,' said Lightfoot. 'We've been searching all over. Come on, the dragon wants to see you.'

In a daze, Rana followed her packmate.

'We have to collect Fenn on the way,' Lightfoot added.

Soon the pair returned to Howling Rock, trotting behind Lightfoot.

Autumn was well underway, and even the magically grown trees of Home Orchard were turning from green to golden. In the late sun, wasps buzzed around the piles of discarded apple cores. Dark grackle birds hopped among the branches, peering at them as they went past. Rana had a strange feeling of the times changing.

The world is not as it was, she said to herself, without really knowing why.

'Welcome back, you two,' said Lyricon. He was just finishing an immense salmon and wiping his face clean of fish juice. Rana noticed that his crystal piles were in disarray, and a section of the tower lay unfinished.

'I'm sorry I was angry,' he said.

'Good!' she said. 'I'm glad that you're sorry. You should be.'

'I haven't been my usual self,' the dragon said. 'Not since the night when—ah . . . the ammolite shattered, anyway. It was a powerful spell. Maybe using so much magic just took it out of me.'

'That makes sense,' agreed Rana.

She hadn't told anyone about the Echo spell, not even Fenn. She was glad Lyricon was being similarly cautious. Catching Fenn's curious tilt of the head, Rana spoke again, before her brother could ask any awkward questions.

'And I'm sorry I didn't tell you I saw you making the miniature tower. I was afraid it was something I shouldn't know about.'

Lyricon sighed. 'It was supposed to be a big surprise for the wolves—including you. After the Seven Fangs let me out of the cage, I wanted to show them other ways my magic could be useful. And a magical firework display seemed a fun idea. Do you know what fireworks are?'

Rana furrowed her brow. 'There is an old story about Fera, the First Wolf, making coloured fire in the sky to celebrate the First Age of wolfkind,' said Rana. 'Is it something like that?'

'Exactly like that.'

Lyricon looked around. 'Is it just the three of us here now?' he asked. At Fenn's nod from the shadows near the entrance, the dragon continued. 'I need to speak to both of you. I have gone off the idea of the big magical firework display. The Seven Fangs *mubbimurkers* have just proved to me that they don't deserve it.'

Rana gave a small smile. Lyricon was sounding a bit more like his old self.

'What happened?' she asked.

He beckoned them closer with a curl of his tail. 'Come nearer, we had better whisper.'

Rana and Fenn crouched with the dragon in the

centre of the room. One tiny rosy crystal glowed in the evening gloom, casting a conspiratorial light.

'First things first.' He raised a sharp claw. 'I can't afford to make the Seven Fangs angry. Did either of you tell any of the other wolves that you thought I was up to something magical or suspicious?'

Both shook their heads.

He sighed with evident relief, then leant forward with a teasing grin. 'Did you promise Sly that my tower would send his name up in lights? Or that it would put on a show of Silver's great-uncle's most interesting diseases?'

Rana smiled. 'Fenn and I only talked about it together,' she replied.

'Good,' said Lyricon. 'Now, let me tell you what is troubling me.' He glanced at the doorway, as if fearing wolfish ears listening there. 'Sly and Silver came in here yesterday, forcing me to help with a new war against the cave lions.'

'Really?' Rana groaned.

'Apparently, the cave lions are scattered and weak. Sly said it was the perfect time to invade their land, and Silver agreed. They told me to create a powerful new golem crystal. They call it the War Crystal. The idea is that any council member can control it and lead an invasion.

'As a prisoner here, I simply couldn't refuse. But in their paws, anywolf they choose could use it to devastating effect. Imagine Sly driving a golem, terrorising all the forest creatures, and not just deadly lions. It is most worrying.'

Rana's heart sank. 'So, they have the crystal. There's no way back.'

'Well,' said Lyricon. 'Perhaps there is . . .'

'There is? What can we do?'

'I know where they've put the War Crystal. My hearing's better than the *mubbimurkers* realise. I heard Silver tell Sly he was studying it in the Cave of Fera.'

Rana recalled the deepest, most sacred cave in Howling Rock; she had been led through it on her first day.

Lyricon produced a beautiful, apple-sized ruby from under his wing and pushed it towards her. 'If you take this gem and touch it to the War Crystal, it will introduce a flaw. The crystal will then crack when they try it out. I'll say that too much power must have caused it to shatter, and tell them that we need to abandon the plan.'

'Brilliant!' said Fenn. Then his nose gave a twitch. 'Er, does it have to be us?'

'You are the only ones I can trust.'

Rana looked thoughtful. Her heart was beating fast. Lyricon trusted them, but could they trust him?

CHAPTER 26

It was the quietest time of the day, when most wolves were asleep. The Seven Fangs had enjoyed their usual big feed and were resting in their chamber; Rana could hear Sly snoring. Nothing could have been more natural than to see Lyricon's helpers trotting around the Rock. They made it down to the ground level unnoticed. It was natural too for Fenn to be fetching and carrying for Rana, and a passing Sunstreak did not look twice at the younger wolf as he passed by with a crystal pouch in his jaws.

'This is it,' whispered Rana when they reached the ground level. Normally, they would trot straight out of the entrance, grateful to be back in the fresh air.

This time they turned right, into the depths of the ancient rock.

They padded softly down the dark passage. The entrance to the Cave of Fera yawned ahead. Rana almost jumped out of her skin as a stray bat flew out of the cave, right between the tips of her ears. As she sprang back with a yelp, Fenn nearly dropped the crystal.

They stood shaking in the silence until they calmed down. At last, they found the courage to creep into the chamber. There was nowolf around. The great image of Fera loomed over them in the rock face above as if watching their every move. Rana bowed her head.

Fenn sneezed. 'My Scent power is itching like crazy. We'd better hurry!'

They peered around the chamber. Then they began to pace back and forth.

'It's not here!' whispered Fenn.

Rana began to panic. Everywhere there were nooks in the rock walls where Sly or Silver could have hidden the War Crystal. Rana sniffed the air. There was a faint smell of the resin Lyricon used to stick crystals together. It led her nose to one of the bigger alcoves. Inside, a large deep-blue sapphire was lying on a dry maple leaf, barely hidden. Her mane tingled as she approached.

'This is it.'

Rana dragged the leaf with her paw and the gemstone shimmered with magical, inner light.

'Just touch the red crystal to the blue,' whispered Fenn.

'I know!'

Rana took the ruby out of the bag with her forepaws. They seemed to be trembling a bit. She paused and looked at Fenn.

'Is it right, what we're doing?' she asked. 'This is loaded with a golem, to help the pack fight our foes—and we are destroying it.'

'Yes! It's right!' said Fenn. 'Do we really want Sly or Silver with a golem under their control? I know what Dad would think about it!'

Rana still did not touch the two crystals. 'All my life I've been taught to run with the pack, to do what the pack want. Now I just don't know!'

Fenn rolled his eyes. 'It's no big deal, Rana. We're not hurting the pack. We're just protecting them from dangerous magic.'

Rana looked down. She wished she could talk to Karla. The old storyteller had warned her what would happen if the Seven Fangs got a taste for dragon magic. Did Rana seriously think another war with the lions would be good for the pack, for the forest? And would the Seven Fangs stop there? Did she trust Sly and Silver more than she trusted Lyricon?

She took a slow, deep breath and contemplated the two crystals. 'What do you think will happen, when they touch?'

'Who knows? You know more about this stuff than I do. Just get on with it!'

Rana sighed, picked up the red crystal and pushed it gently but firmly against the blue.

For a moment, all was silent.

Then, *BOOM*.

Everything happened at once. The blue crystal shattered with a sound like thunder, foul smoke filled the air—and a voice rang out across the chamber.

'There they are! The traitors!'

Ela stood in the doorway, with Silver and Sly behind her.

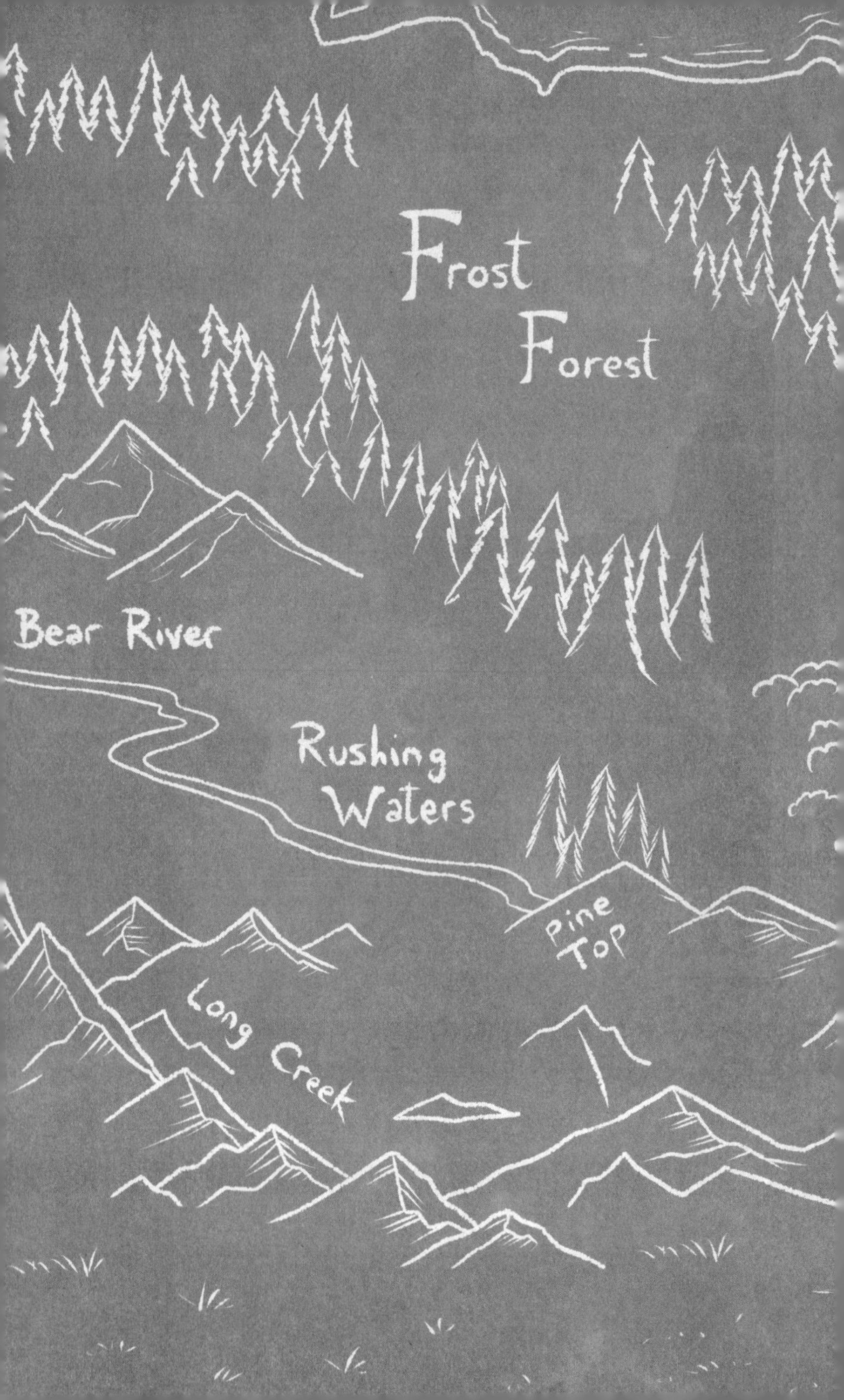

Frost Forest
Bear River
Rushing Waters
Pine Top
Long Creek

Part Three:

The Dragons

CHAPTER 27

'How do you plead?'

'Guilty,' Rana said, quietly. 'Of trying to stop the pack making a big mistake,' she added.

'You will suffer for this!' said Sly.

They had been marched to Dragon Cave to answer to the Seven Fangs. Their father was absent, still away with Karla at Spook Bay. But the other pack leaders, with their lieutenants and favoured warriors, gathered around. Lyricon sat in silence, like a great sleeping serpent on a rock, Ela by his side.

'Ela, what made you suspect that an attempt might be made to sabotage the crystal?' asked Silver.

'It was Lyricon,' she said. 'He was worried that

something like this would happen. By wolves that are against the Great Pack.'

Rana gazed in disbelief at Ela. Then at Lyricon.

How could that be possible? Was Ela lying? Would Lyricon speak up for them?

'What do you say, Lyricon?' asked Silver.

'Rana is definitely against the idea of attacking the cave lions,' said the dragon. 'She also knows how all my crystals work. She could easily have stolen this red crystal and used it to destroy the new golem. A terrible act of betrayal . . .' he stopped speaking, as if overcome with emotion.

Rana was too shocked to speak. She looked around desperately for a friend in the chamber. Sunstreak met her gaze, impassive. Fenn was trembling and staring ahead, as if overwhelmed by events.

'Lyricon told us to do it!' he blurted out.

'Ridiculous!' snorted Sly.

Rana's mind was a whir of confusion. But there was one thing she was suddenly very sure of. A truth that had to come out.

'The Victory Tower is not what it seems,' Rana growled. 'The dragon is making something magical, and keeping its true purpose secret.'

'Yes, my Scent says so too! Ask him about that!' yelped Fenn.

'Silence!' roared Sly.

'Absurd!' scoffed Silver. 'It seems this pair will say anything to save their scraggy fur.'

Lyricon looked sad. 'They have long been opposed to the ambitions of the Great Pack,' he said. 'I had hoped to win them over. Alas, it seems I failed.'

'Traitors!' came a howl from a warrior at the back.

'A traitor should be ripped apart!' snarled Sly. A few more warriors barked in agreement.

Sunstreak was grave. 'Rana has served us well until now. I will not see her come to harm—even if she is misguided.'

'It might not be up to you!' Sly bared his teeth. 'We can't have traitors in the pack!'

Silver looked worried. 'But we cannot slay the daughter of Darkmane!'

Lyricon rose up, his one good wing spreading out as he towered over the wolves. 'Stop!' he cried, casting a shadow across the room. 'It is very bad luck for a dragon to let his apprentice be harmed,' he said. 'It would bring a curse down on us all. Rana and her brother must be exiled, sent far away!'

'Exile!' Sly nodded slowly. 'That's just what they deserve.'

In a state of shock, Rana and Fenn were marched out of Howling Rock while warriors were summoned to accompany them to the border.

In a brief visit, Rana and Fenn were allowed to say goodbye to their mother. Boulder, their guard, hung back to let them speak in private.

After initial disbelief, Ayala managed to remain calm. 'The whole thing smells like a dead skunk!' she growled. 'But I can't leave the cubs to fight all seven packs over this. Darkmane and I will sort it out together when he comes home. Promise me you'll look after each other until then.' She nuzzled Rana. 'You've become somewolf, Daughter, dealing with the dragon and the Seven Fangs every day. You can't imagine how the pack like to talk about you! You've grown to become canny and brave. You can survive this.'

Her mother turned to give Fenn one last lick as Rana blinked away tears at the unexpected praise.

Then suddenly, an idea struck her. Rana sprang up, went to Karla's corner of the den and with the point of one of her claws, scratched a spiral shape in the soft earth.

At an impatient bark from Boulder, it was time to go. Rana and Fenn were accompanied by two wolves from Stalker pack, Temper and Prowl, who were ordered not to talk to them. Soon, they began the long lope away from Howling Rock. It was a dismal trek with no speaking allowed, no rest stops and no breaks to hunt.

The closest border was the great grassland plain at the foot of the Tumbledown Scree, where the Mountains of the Dawn ended. When they reached the final piece of solid rock before the great green space began, Temper and Prowl came to a halt. They peered out into the mysterious expanse of wilderness, then looked down at the two smaller wolves.

'You are hereby exiled from Hunter's Reach,' Temper said. 'If you are ever seen again on any land belonging to the Great Pack, you will be shown no mercy.'

Rana surprised herself by feeling no fear. Her sense of justice was stronger. 'You are making a big mistake,' she said. 'And it will come back to bite you.'

'Go,' said Temper and turned away.

Both guards sprang up into the jumble of rocks and soon disappeared.

Rana and Fenn stared out into that great sea of grass that swished and swayed in the wind.

'I'm sorry.' Rana sighed.

Fenn looked at her. 'Sorry?'

'Sorry I got you into this. If I hadn't agreed to be Lyricon's spokeswolf, then you would never have—'

'Forget all that!' Fenn replied. 'If you hadn't got me mixed up in dragon business, then you'd probably be doing this exile alone—and then you *would* be in trouble!' He narrowed his eyes as he peered ahead. 'I'm more worried at the moment about snakes,' he added, eyeing the long grass suspiciously, his nose twitching.

'So?' replied Rana. 'We're not going that way.'

'Where are we going?'

'About five minutes' trot along the edge of the plain,' said Rana. 'Then straight back into Hunter's Reach.'

'Is this a good idea?' asked Fenn, his ears flat and his tail drooping low.

'Come on!' barked Rana. The rain poured from a slate-grey sky, and wild wind tossed the tops of the trees. The cry of a raven split the air.

'They said that we would be torn apart if we were ever found here again!'

'Well, we won't be found, will we? We are too clever for that.'

Thunder rolled around the hills and ravines as the pair loped through the barren canyons on the edge of the wolves' realm. They cut west across the outliers of the Mountains of the Dawn, so as to avoid the guards who had just left them.

Several hours later, they sheltered under some bent thorn trees by a narrow brook. Fenn managed to catch a couple of small voles for them to make a meal.

'What do you make of it all?' Fenn asked. 'Were we caught red-pawed by chance? Was Lyricon forced to lie to save his own skin?'

Rana frowned. 'I think there's more to it than that,' she said. 'I need time to think. But I do have a bit of a plan.'

'A plan?' Fenn looked pleased. 'You might have told me earlier,' he added. 'I've been coming up with dozens! But let's hear yours first.'

'Before we left,' Rana said, 'I needed to let Karla know where we were going, so she could find us. There's a secret place we can hide, really close to Starlight pack territory. And only Karla knows it's there.'

'But you couldn't talk to her. She wasn't there. How will she know where we're going?'

Rana smiled. 'I'll show you.'

They kept going through the night. As they loped along a low valley, the moon briefly appeared in a break in the cloud. High on a ridge they saw the dark silhouette of a cougar. The powerful shoulders, long neck and rather small, but alert, head were unmistakable. The sight froze their blood. Even Darkmane would lose a scrap with one of those.

The creature did not look their way, but sprang off into the shadows of a distant gully. Such threats were scarce in those parts, but never far from a wolf's thoughts. Sticking to the deep gloom of the lower valleys, they made a wide circle, downwind of the predator.

'We were lucky that time,' whispered Fenn. 'You see how chancy it is being out of the pack.'

Rana noticed how stressed he was and forgot about her own fear. 'Fera is with us,' she said. 'We will continue to be lucky.'

They were not lucky with the weather, however. Damp, cold and exhausted, they finally came to a mountain slope that overlooked a thick pine forest. To Fenn, the area seemed barren and uninviting. A large cave yawned in the rock wall.

'Sorry about the long lope,' panted Rana. After a quick sniff of the cave mouth, she stood just inside it and shook a day's worth of rain out of her fur.

'Is this it?' Fenn looked unimpressed. 'Your secret place we came so far to find? It looks like a damp hole.'

Rana had already vanished inside. 'This hole has a surprise,' she called back. She sprang up some rocks, her eyes scanning the walls in the gloom. There was just enough light to see the shape that had haunted her dreams. A vast spiral loomed above her, carved—or melted—into the wall.

Rana felt the same awe she had first experienced in the presence of the shape. Glancing back, she saw Fenn was gazing with a quizzical look.

‘What is it?’ he whispered. The spiral inspired a kind of caution, almost as if it might hear you talking about it.

‘An ancient sign of some kind. Maybe even made by dragons. Karla showed me it not long ago—before the shooting star came and turned all our lives upside down. I scratched a copy of this sign by her place in the den. Nowolf else will know what it is.’

Fenn scented the air. He peered around as if expecting a dragon to jump out at him from under a rock. ‘There is definitely something weird about this place,’ he said. ‘It’s so quiet.’

‘Maybe the magic of the dragons and the Far-off Times lingers in the air. Karla said no creatures come here, so we should be safe to use it as a shelter. Sooner or later she will get my message, I’m sure—’

She was cut off as a great boom of thunder shook the hills.

‘I’ve never seen it so stormy!’ said Fenn. ‘Thunder never scares me, of course. I rather like it.’ A slight quiver in his limbs seemed to say otherwise.

‘Everything looks worse without your pack around you,’ said Rana. ‘Makes you realise how lucky you are to be a member. Even the annoying ones are part of your strength in a way.'

'Except now we aren't in a pack,' said Fenn. 'And the annoying ones—like Ela and Sly—have cast us out.'

Rana looked thoughtful. 'I don't know that Ela deliberately caused us trouble,' she said after a while. 'I really think she believed she was just helping the pack.'

There was another crash of thunder, sending a wave of echoes through the valley that seemed to go on forever.

'We're in a right mess, this time.' Fenn sighed. 'Just saying. I wonder what Dad will think of it. Plus, I miss my supply of top-quality salmon. I used to pinch a bit of Lyricon's dinner when it arrived.'

'No wonder he hated you,' said Rana, with a grin.

Fenn looked puzzled. 'But I thought he *loved* you,' he said. 'You basically saved his life. Probably more than once. That's what I can't understand about all this.'

His remark seemed to plunge Rana into silence. For a long time, the pair just sat watching the storm. The wind was changing direction and now the rain was almost horizontal, blowing into the cave.

'Just when you thought things couldn't get any worse,' said Fenn, chilly and damp.

'It might be a bit cosier further inside,' said Rana, snooping about. 'Let's sniff around.'

They padded cautiously inside. The cave went on and on, more like a tunnel into the mountain.

'I never saw a cave like this before,' said Fenn. He stopped. They had both noticed a faint glow ahead. 'Look, it gets lighter. Maybe it leads out to another cave?'

'Except we're going into the mountainside and downwards,' replied Rana, 'and this glow is more like moonlight than daylight.'

Cautiously, they pressed on. Now they could see a small blur of light ahead, an opening into . . . something.

'How is your super Scent doing?' asked Rana. 'Is it safe?' She had to admit, her brother's ability was coming in handy, and she no longer treated it like a family joke.

'It feels safe,' said Fenn. 'Of course, my danger Scent isn't infallible. Remember when we were cubs, I once stepped into a stagnant bog and stank for a week.'

'Very reassuring,' said Rana.

The tunnel had taken them to what appeared to be the entrance to a bigger chamber.

'It feels OK,' whispered Fenn. 'I'll go in.'

Rana waited as Fenn vanished into the next cave. Moments later, there was a terrific yelp.

'Rana!'

'Fenn!' she cried, bounding after him.

Inside, a terrifying scene lay before them. The chamber was full of bones—wolf bones. Fenn was staring, astonished, at the spectacle. The skeletons lay in startled attitudes, as if overcome by some sudden fate in a time long gone. Skulls peered with dark, hollow eyes. Rib cages were overgrown with a thin, grey ivy that seemed to have crawled in from a brighter chamber beyond.

'It's . . . it's like an ancient graveyard!' whispered Fenn. 'Cool!'

Rana made a face. 'Cool? More like creepy. This must be the site of some terrible tragedy. Maybe we should go back.'

'No,' said Fenn. 'The Scent says it's safe. Whatever happened here can't hurt us now! And up ahead, I'm smelling something . . . good.'

As they crept through the weird tomb of ancient skeletons, new odours were reaching their noses: rich, fertile, complex, like the deep forest in midsummer. The pair almost sprinted to the entrance of the next chamber they had discovered.

Fenn spoke first. 'Er . . . wow.'

CHAPTER 28

Rana never forgot the wonder she felt as she gazed upon the incredible sight for the first time. She and Fenn stood on the edge of a vast underground cavern. As far as the eye could see, a beautiful subterranean forest stretched before them.

'What is this place?' gasped Rana. All around them, unknown plants spread enormous leaves. Flowers dangled from creepers, huge toadstools rose like towers, and familiar trees like cottonwood, spruce and oak sprawled in stunted forms. Deep moss gardens filled underground canyons with luxurious growth. Here and there, small birds darted and whistled; butterflies twinkled by on brilliant wings.

In the distance, they could now see the source of the light, a glowing mist—possibly covering a lake or pool far away in the centre. As they padded along, they discovered fruit trees, cherries and apples, in abundance. Fat, flightless birds—for which they had no name—waddled out of the brush here and there. Frogs plopped in the pools; little voles and other furry critters scuttled about their business.

'We can hunt here, and no-one from the Great Pack will find us!' said Fenn.

'But what's causing that glowing mist?' wondered Rana.

'Let's worry about that another day,' said Fenn. 'Right now, I'm starving.'

The discovery of the secret land had filled their hearts with wonder and raised their spirits. Rejuvenated, they made short work of catching a couple of the plump waddling birds. They sat on a mossy bank, chewing happily as they peered at their strange new world.

'It looks like we've found our larder,' said Fenn. 'At last, things are looking up!'

The soft glow in the great cavern created a feeling of timelessness. The wolves no longer knew if it was day or night. They did know they were exhausted, however, and found a high, moss-covered ridge to rest in.

'I'll take first watch,' yawned Fenn. In a short while, they were both asleep.

A sudden whistling of chickadee birds woke them. For a moment, Rana reached out with her snout to touch her mother, Ayala, and instead found her nose in a pile of moss. The whole calamity of the past days came back to her in an instant. Her heart filled with dismay, but she was determined not to show it to Fenn. She sprang up.

'Wake up!' She gave him a prod with a forepaw. 'Your personal larder is waiting for you,' she said. The pair were soon trotting through the underground forest.

'How long do we have?' asked Fenn.

'What do you mean?'

'I mean, before we have to return to the cave? If that's where Karla will look for us.'

'She is away with Darkmane at Spook Bay,' said Rana. 'We have a couple of days, at least, before she sees my secret sign, if not more. After that, one of us will have to be at the spiral cave all the time, on watch.'

'So, for now,' said Fenn, 'we have plenty of time to explore.'

Bounding through a meadow of little white flowers, Rana came to a sudden halt.

'Uh-oh,' she said. 'Look.' There on the track ahead was a pile of bones.

'Deer,' said Fenn. 'Tasty!'

'Yes,' said Rana. 'But whatever finds deer tasty might find us tasty too. We have to exercise maximum vigilance until we know.'

'You sound like Darkmane,' said Fenn. 'Are you taking charge? We are a pack of two now. I think it might be best. Gripper always says I'll make a brilliant lieutenant. I'm a natural second-in-command, apparently.'

They padded along in silence now. Rana immediately drew Fenn's attention to some smashed shrubs near the feeding site. In that untouched haven, the passage of one large creature was not hard to detect—a broken stalk here, a scratch mark on a toadstool trunk there . . .

Rana paused to sniff some freshly scraped tree-bark. 'Smells like bear, a male, I think.'

'Let's take the high road,' whispered Fenn. 'We want to spot this guy before he spots us.'

They loped silently along one of the stone ridges that ran through the cavern.

'There!' said Rana. Down below, perched on a rock by a little underground stream, one paw snatching for fish, was a very big, very old bear. Rana immediately recognised the familiar shape.

'Greyface!'

'Just our luck,' groaned Fenn. At that moment, the great grizzly turned and saw them. Fenn nudged Rana with his flank, urging her away.

'I'll go and talk to him,' said Rana.

'You'll what?'

Remembering her most respectful body language, Rana sidled towards him in a diagonal path, her face averted. Greyface ignored her and continued to fish. Recalling Karla's advice about speaking to other species—that flattery and good manners helped—she used the politest words she knew to speak to the bear, and voiced them as slowly and clearly as possible.

'Oh, Great Bear,' she began awkwardly.

'Hmph!' Greyface snorted rudely.

'Wise king of the woods,' she added. Greyface stopped fishing. He turned slowly on the rock, to avoid slipping into the stream. Rana moved closer, taking care to remain well out of paw's reach.

'Lord of this paradise,' she added.

'That's more like it,' he said.

'Oh, Great Greyface, enemy of none!' she continued. She spoke a little more confidently now. The bear peered down at her, seeming less grumpy.

'She-wolf,' he grunted. 'I have smelled you before.'

'I am Rana, friend of Karla.'

'I see,' he replied. 'Well, Rana friend of Karla, get lost.'

'What's happening?' called Fenn, from the nearby underbrush.

'He's telling me to get lost,' Rana hissed back.

'Good idea,' said Fenn.

'What is this place?' Rana asked.

'This is my secret place!' growled Greyface. 'Few come here.'

'Does it have a name?'

'Some call it the Under-Reach,' said Greyface.

'Others call it Ungoria—but that is a very old name from the Far-off Times.'

'How can there be a forest underground?'

'The birds say the magic comes from the glowing pool,' said Greyface.

'So how—'

'No more questions!' roared the bear. 'Wolves are not wanted here. Even polite ones. The secret place is very good for Greyface to live in, now that he is old and does not want trouble.'

'I'm not bringing any trouble,' said Rana.

'Good,' grunted Greyface. 'I will call you Bråha—Young-but-wise.' He rose and pointed with a great dark paw. 'Now go back home to your tower of rock!'

Rana did not move. She simply stared for a moment. Fenn pulled her by the tail with his front teeth. 'Come on, you've been dismissed.'

But Rana did not move straight away. She looked to the side, her eyes narrowing. Suddenly, she sprang up and raced off.

CHAPTER 29

'Where are we going?' asked Fenn, struggling to keep up with Rana.

'Didn't you notice?' Rana asked. 'When Greyface told us to go back to Howling Rock, he didn't point back the way we came . . . he pointed the other way—*this* way.'

'So?'

'So, look—there's another hole in the wall, just where he pointed. That's where he thinks we've come from.'

'But he's wrong.'

'Yes, but *why* does he think we came that way? Maybe he knows something.'

'You mean it could be—'

'Another passage, yes!'

The wolves had another meal—the waddle-birds were *very* tasty—before tackling the new passage.

'Are you sure this is a good idea?' Fenn asked, as they set off into the echoing gloom. 'We already found a great hideaway.'

'Yes, but if there's a tunnel that leads home, we have to know,' said Rana. 'I'd like to see them exile me then! We could spy on the pack, see our friends, come and go as we please.'

Fenn sighed. 'I kind of liked the hiding. We were getting really good at it.'

'I know,' said Rana. 'But we can't just do nothing. Lyricon is up to something. And whatever it is, I think it's going to happen very soon. The pack are going to need us, I'm sure of it.'

'Didn't I hear Greyface give you a name? What's that all about?'

'I'll have to ask Karla,' said Rana, secretly pleased. 'I'm Bråha now in bear language. It might turn out to be a good thing.'

'Having a bear name is probably considered

traitorous by Sly too,' said Fenn, although with a grin. 'You'll probably get double-exiled over it and have to live on the moon!'

They both laughed as they explored the tunnel. The passage that Greyface had pointed to was a wide, clear one, with few rockfalls or narrow spaces. Ahead they heard a low rushing sound, and caught the scent of fresh water.

'There's something funny about these caves,' said Rana. 'They are too smooth. They look—I don't know—made on purpose, like the spiral in the wall.'

'This Under-Reach is full of surprises,' said Fenn. 'And look, here's another.'

Turning a bend in the rock, they came upon a deep underground stream flowing swiftly along the side of the passage.

'OK, let's see how far this passage goes,' said Rana.

'Another long lope?' Fenn pulled a face. 'Really?'

Rana looked ahead, thoughtful. She began to scramble down the rocky bank to the dark stream. 'Maybe not,' she said. 'Let's swim!'

The wolves cautiously stepped into the cool water. It was easily deep enough to swim in, and carried them on with a gentle but rapid motion.

'Ha ha, this is easier than running everywhere,' said Fenn. 'I like this place. And you're full of good ideas, Rana. I'm glad you're my leader.'

At first, they stayed close to the sides, in case they needed to exit the stream quickly. Gradually, the pair came to trust that no lurking crocodiles lay in wait for them, although the occasional water snake could be seen wriggling by. They did not even come across any sudden rapids or waterfalls, just a smooth, easy flow through the darkness. Occasionally, a shaft high above shed a little light in the deep gloom. At one point, the stream hurried through some wide stepping stones that crossed the water.

'These will be fun to leap if we have to walk back,' said Fenn. 'See how the path changes from one side of the tunnel to the other.'

'Of course, we'll have to walk back,' said Rana. 'We can't go against the current. Enjoy the ride while you can.'

The flow took them for many miles. In fact, Rana was growing a little anxious at just how far they were travelling, when she spotted a bright light up ahead. The drumming of deep echoes revealed that they had reached a cavern where the tunnel came to an end. Light peeped down from a hole above. Glad to get out of the chilly water, they both scrambled onto a stony shore.

'The stream must vanish further below ground here,' said Rana. 'Let's see where we are.'

'We were in the water for ages,' said Fenn. 'We're probably in Wilderland now.'

They shook themselves dry and began to explore. But there was a disappointment. The sides of the pit they were in overhung them sharply. There was no obvious way to climb out. They tried to run, leap and clamber up the sides, but it was no good.

'I give up,' groaned Fenn. 'I'm exhausted!'

A final desperate scramble by Rana resulted in her reaching a sort of halfway point, a narrow ledge of rock sticking out of the wall of dried clay.

'I think I've split one of my claws,' she said, sucking her paw.

'You sound like Ela,' said Fenn. 'What can you see?'

Rana peered up. 'I think I know where we are!' she said. Her cry echoed around the pit. 'I recognise the trees.'

'Rana, there are trees of all kinds everywhere!'

Fenn laughed. 'I know you have a reputation for being observant . . .'

'Come and see for yourself.'

Fenn tried to join her but could not manage the climb. 'I give up,' he said, flopping on the ground. 'You're the great storyteller. Describe what you see.'

'These aren't just any trees. There are some tall pines in old Starlight territory that were struck by lightning. One is split in half and completely black. Most of the branches hang down in a funny way. It can only be one place, Thunder Edge. It's not far from Howling Rock at all. As cubs, we were actually warned against coming here—don't you remember? Because of the bottomless pit. Now we're in it!'

'Well, at least we know it's not bottomless,' said Fenn. 'But it's not much use to us, either, if we can't get up. I wonder how old Greyface got in?'

'There might be many ways into Ungoria if you know where to look. But this has turned out to be a dead end.'

Feeling defeated and utterly exhausted, the pair flopped down. As they were far from anywhere they could call home, they decided that one of them would watch while the other slept. Rana volunteered to take the first watch, but the echoing of the waters around the pit kept Fenn awake for a long time. After just a couple of hours, they swapped over. Although her body ached from all their travels, Rana felt restless.

'Will you stop all that pacing around?' she said. Fenn had been padding in circles as the gathering twilight began to fill the pit with shadow.

'It's the Scent,' muttered Fenn. 'My nose is telling me we should head back to the spiral cave. Maybe we'll sleep better there.'

So, barely rested, they decided to head back. As the current was against the wolves this time, swimming was out. A long, tiring lope awaited them.

It took a lot longer than either had expected to return to Ungoria. In fact, it felt like they had been walking forever. When they reached the leafy sanctuary of the main chamber, the soft light of the misty pool felt like the sun in springtime. Looking down from a clover-covered rise, Rana remembered *The Tale of Firemane the Fierce* and the magic pool he discovered. Could it possibly be . . . ?

She was too tired to think about it now. They stopped for a rest and slept longer than they intended before making their way back to the cave they temporarily called home. The sun was sinking in the sky when they returned. They sat in the mouth of the cave, peering across the tops of the pines and chewing on the bones of a plump waddle-bird.

'Time is running out,' said Rana. 'If only we knew what was happening at Howling Rock. It's full moon tomorrow . . . Victory Day. I've got a bad feeling about it.'

'Yes.' Fenn sighed. 'Even if Lyricon's not planning some sneaky magical tower, those idiots Sly and Silver will declare war on the cave lions, get a new dragon golem, and we will probably never know peace again.'

Rana suddenly sprang to her feet. 'Look!'

She pointed with her snout. Glimpsed through pine trunks on a slope below, a narrow shape was moving fast and casting a long, flowing shadow in the afternoon sun.

'Karla?' Fenn asked.

It was heading straight towards them. It was moving too fast, and it was far too big to be the old she-wolf.

'What shall we do?' Fenn asked.

Rana studied the new arrival closely and her ears sprang up. Her tail began to swish from side to side. She sat down again. 'We wait.'

A dark wolf with a great shaggy mane and fiery eyes appeared in the mouth of the cave, silhouetted against the glare of the sun.

'Dad!' yelped Fenn.

'So here you are, my little traitors,' Darkmane said, looking them over. 'None the worse for wear, by the looks of it. In fact, quite well fed.' He peered at the bones they had been chewing.

'Where's Karla?' asked Rana.

'She told me where to come,' Darkmane said. 'I can run a lot faster than her, and we needed to know you were safe. Besides, I want to hear all about your exile.'

Fenn looked at Rana. 'It's story time,' he said. 'You're on, sis!'

Rana collected her thoughts. 'Stories should start at the beginning,' she said. 'And I think it all began to go wrong when I saw Lyricon's so-called artwork, the Victory Tower . . .'

As the sun went down over the pines, Rana told

the whole tale. As he listened, Darkmane's expression turned from astonishment to deep concern. At the end, he rose and stood looking back in the direction of Howling Rock.

'This is all deeply troubling,' he growled. 'Lyricon is up to something, and I think all his crystals should be removed and magic plans stopped until we can get to the bottom of it. The problem is, it is just my voice—and possibly Sunstreak's—against the other five pack leaders. They all think that the dragon is going to give us victory over the cave lions and bring on a golden age for wolves.'

'What can we do?' asked Fenn.

'The good thing is that you are safe, my children,' said Darkmane. 'I can leave you here, for now, and race back to the Rock. If I confront the dragon—'

'You can't face Lyricon alone, Dad!' said Rana. 'He's tricky. Only Fenn and I really know what he's capable of.'

'And only Rana might know how to stop him,' said Fenn. 'She practically does all the magic with him.'

The older wolf narrowed his eyes. 'You do know him the best, that's true,' he agreed.

But Rana could see her father was on the verge of leaving without them. It went against his instincts to put them in danger. But she could not back down. Something in her heart refused to be left out of the action now. She had to show him that she was not the cautious cub that hid behind the elk antlers any longer.

Rana stepped forward and bowed her head low. 'Pack leader,' she said, in a quiet but determined voice, 'knowledge of this dragon and its magic is my strength. My strength is there to help the pack. It is yours to command.'

Darkmane nodded slowly. 'Well spoken, Storyteller. Perhaps there is a truth here only you can uncover. Besides, we can't leave Fenn in this cave all alone . . .'

CHAPTER 30

It was the largest gathering in the history of the wolves. Apart from one border patrol, every member of the Great Pack had been summoned to Howling Rock to hear the plans for the future.

From the Snowfoot pack, many yearlings came down from the mountains for the first time ever, to meet their brothers and sisters of the Great Pack. Also, Karla had returned with the Horizon pack scouts, who patrolled the northern border. All were drawn to the centre of the wolf realm to see such famous names as Silver, Sly and Darkmane, whose heroic deeds had been spread in stories far and wide across Hunter's Reach.

The Seven Fangs were gathering on a long ledge above the main entrance to Howling Rock. It was the perfect vantage point from which to address the crowd.

Silver surveyed the view, anticipating the impact of his great speech later. His thoughts were troubled, however, by the feeling that all was not going as planned.

'Where is Sly?' Silver asked. 'Where is Darkmane? This is not the time for council members to start vanishing.'

Sly suddenly appeared behind him. 'And what is going on in Dragon Cave?' he asked. 'I wanted to check up on Lyricon, but the dratted dragon has shut himself in.'

'He has *what*?'

'He's blocked the entrance with more rocks. It's most peculiar.'

Just then, Ela joined them. 'It's alright,' she said. 'I got Boulder to help with it. Lyricon asked for complete solitude. He's utterly exhausted after finishing the work on the Victory Tower. Solitude is a dragon thing, apparently.'

Silver frowned. 'Rather irregular, but we can't

worry about it now.' He turned away and watched the packs gathering below. 'The whole council should be here,' he muttered. 'I wonder what Darkmane is up to?'

It was a more difficult journey than Rana had expected. The storms of the previous days had left a mudslide at Bear River Pass, forcing them to spend all night going the long way, through Knotty Pine Gorge. Here, Fenn had trodden on a thorn and needed attention.

Tired and pawsore by early morning, they had finally taken a deep trail through ancient forest in old Starlight Pack territory to a rocky overhang, where the three felt safe enough to shelter from the midday sun.

It was a winding way home from their resting place, but the trail would take them right where they needed to be, within a short sprint of Howling Rock, unseen. Night was falling when they resumed their trek, however, and there was still some way to go.

The full moon was rising above the Mountains of the Dawn, and a hush fell over the pack. As far as the eye could see, around Howling Rock, under the eaves of Home Orchard, and perched on rocks in the distance, wolves were assembled.

'We can't wait for Darkmane any longer,' said Silver. 'We shall have to go ahead without full council.'

Sly agreed. 'He has been sulking ever since we exiled his children. Perhaps in the future, we will have to do many things without full council.'

He and Silver exchanged a long look, then they both moved to the front of the ledge to address the Great Pack.

'Brothers and sisters, kin of blood and fur,' cried Silver. 'Today is a great day for wolf-kind!' An excited howl went up from the horde of wolves.

'We have declared it Victory Day,' roared Sly, 'as all our foes are defeated, and live trembling in fear of our power!'

There were more yelps of delight.

'To commemorate this great day, our dragon ally has created a special monument to show our glory to the world.'

He nodded at Ela, who howled up to Dragon Cave. This was the signal for Lyricon to reveal his sculpture. Unseen worker wolves pulled on vines. Levers and pulleys made by Lyricon creaked and turned. Before the eyes of the crowd, the gleaming tower rose up, pointing to the sky. Its crystals reflected the bright glow of the rising moon, making it stand out against the night. There was a low 'Ooh' from the crowd.

Sly looked on with satisfaction, then returned to his speech. 'Greatest of all,' he said, 'is the next news. Perhaps you have heard rumours. Perhaps you have had hopes. I am here to tell you now, we are declaring war on the cave lions, and—'

Sly paused. He was not receiving quite the attention he expected. Instead of all eyes being on him, they were still gazing upwards. The tower was shining more brightly now and sending little bolts of light up into the sky. The sounds of awe from the crowd were growing.

'Wow!'

'That *is* amazing!'

The bolts of light grew bigger. The light brighter.

Now, everywolf was looking up, and none had eyes on Sly or any of the other Seven Fangs. The lights began to turn into rings of fire that grew larger, spreading outwards. High into the night they soared, visible for miles. Some wolves began to turn away from the blinding glare. Vibrations from the tower were beginning to shake Howling Rock, causing loose rocks to tumble down the sides.

A short distance away, Rana looked on. The three wolves had just arrived in the canyon that led to Howling Rock.

'What is your friend doing?' growled Darkmane.

'That is not a celebration display,' said Rana. 'It's a beacon—a signal of some kind. And it's serious magic. He has to be stopped!'

By now, the pack had stopped cheering. In fact, it had fallen eerily quiet.

An ominous feeling gripped the wolves. The pulsing from the tower had grown so strong that it could even be felt through the ground. The youngest cubs cowered together, their ears flat, whimpering. A narrow ledge about halfway up Howling Rock began to crack, showering stones and huge clods of earth onto the wolves below. There were yelps of pain as some were struck by the debris. The wolves began to scatter, seeking safety.

At the next great pulse from the tower, stones

showered down on the ledge where the Seven Fangs were standing. By now, the night sky was practically on fire with the dazzling glare of the bright rings that flared and faded, one upon another.

'Get up there and stop him!' roared Silver. There was a sudden panic among the council wolves. Chiggers, Sly and Sunstreak raced up to Dragon Cave, only to be faced with a wall of rubble.

'Of course, the beast's shut itself in!' said Sly. 'Break it down!'

In moments, several of the strongest warriors were shoving at the rocks with their forepaws.

'Rana tried to warn us about this,' said Sunstreak. 'At the trial—she said Lyricon was up to something.'

'I have a feeling,' said Sly, 'that we've been tricked.'

Rana was already racing across the canyon with Darkmane at her side. Fenn was at their heels. She looked up in awe at the soaring rings of light. Lyricon had done all this? It was powerful magic.

She darted through the chaotic ranks of the Great Pack. Darkmane's presence helped her cut through the nervous throng. Soon, she was at the main entrance to Howling Rock, where the Seven Fangs were now gathered. Silver had a wild look in his yellow eyes. Everywolf turned to look at the new arrivals.

'Exiles! How dare you show your faces here!' said Sly.

'Rana is here under my protection,' growled Darkmane. He stood before the council, his hackles raised, his teeth bared. 'She warned you all that Lyricon was up to something, and you didn't listen. Now stand aside!'

Rana raced up the familiar route to Dragon Cave. Even with the walls around them shuddering and shaking, the warriors had made quick work of the rubble blocking the entry, but they were stumped by what they found inside.

'We're in!' called Gripper. 'But we don't know what to do!'

Rana scrambled over the heap of stones at the entrance. The chamber floor was completely covered in rows of crystals radiating in a spiral pattern from a vast purple amethyst in the centre. Incense was burning in hollow gourds placed around the cave, filling the chamber with the heady fragrance of sage and juniper. The scene was lit at regular intervals by the dazzling flashes from outside.

The wolves gazed around the shadow-streaked room and one thing became apparent.

'He's escaped!'

There was no sign of Lyricon anywhere.

'Break up the patterns!' shouted Rana. 'Quickly! We must stop the signal!'

'Patterns?' Chiggers looked confused.

'The crystals! Just scatter them!'

Rana began to scrabble at the coloured gems with her front paws. 'Don't leave any rows intact. Break up any sequence of colours that is repeated!'

The other wolves frantically copied her actions. Fenn darted here and there to check that no patterns remained.

Soon, they could feel a change in the air. The cave gradually stopped vibrating. The flashes from outside started to fade in intensity.

'Rana, you are a genius,' said Darkmane. 'You've stopped it!'

'We've broken the spell,' said Rana. 'But are we too late? I don't know. Those lights must have been seen from here to Spook Bay. Maybe even the Barren Isles, for all we know. That was obviously what Lyricon intended . . .'

'You've saved Howling Rock, anyway,' her father said. 'The whole place was about to fall down. We were just in time.'

'We have to find Lyricon,' said Sly. 'He must have somehow got out of one of the window cracks. He might even be on top of the rock right now!'

The wolves raced out. In the rush, no-one noticed that Rana stayed exactly where she was. Now that the bright glow had stopped, the room was gloomy in the pale moonlight. The scuffed, discarded gemstones and ruined incense gave the place an air of catastrophe.

'You can show yourself now,' said Rana.

There was a stirring in the shadows and—out of nothing, so it seemed—the dragon appeared, faint, like a ghostly presence. His face was long and his scales grey with exhaustion. His eyes were like pools of darkness.

'How did you guess?'

'I know you can't get out. And I know you can do invisibility spells . . . for a limited time. And you don't need gourds of fancy incense to do your magic. I figured you were burning it to hide your smell, so nowolf could sniff you out.'

Lyricon was now fully visible again. Yet even in the drastic circumstances, Rana was shocked to see him so drained of life.

'You are not supposed to be here,' he said, his voice a broken whisper. 'I made sure you were sent away.'

'Why? What have you done?'

'Called for help,' said Lyricon. 'I have to escape. Could you live in a cramped hole with the threat of death hanging over you every day?' He gestured around at the wrecked chamber and almost fell over. Taking a long breath, he steadied himself. 'Rana, I'm young—full of hopes, dreams! Like you, I have hardly lived yet. I can't wake up every night with the fear of wolf teeth at my neck!'

For the first time, he showed the full depth of the desperation and fear he had been hiding so well during his captivity. Rana felt pity for him.

'You could have told me what you were doing,' she said. 'I would have understood. Why did you have to pull that trick?'

'Told you my plan? Then you would have had to stop me. Your loyalty is to your pack. I had to get you out of the way.'

'Out of the way of what?'

Lyricon did not reply. He looked beyond her, out into the night sky. He had the air of someone waiting for something.

'I thought we were friends!' Rana cried. 'Beyond matters of dragons and wolves! I thought we were friends—just you and me.'

Lyricon continued to stare out at the darkness. Rana heard cries from the crowd below.

'Look! The stars! The stars are falling!'

Darkmane was calling her. 'Rana, come quickly! Look at this!'

As she rushed to the door, she called back to Lyricon, 'You are not going anywhere!'

'Really?' came the reply. 'We shall see. But you must fly—fly for your life, or . . .'

Lyricon's reply was never finished. Unseen by Rana, his feeble body slumped to the floor amidst the ruined patterns of crystal.

Rana was already outside. She had raced down to join the wolves at the foot of the rock. They were all staring up into the sky. The magic tower had gone dark, but the sky had not returned to normal. It was filled with shooting stars, dropping in their direction. Some were tinged with ruddy flame.

'Is it part of his magic?' asked Darkmane. She could not answer. A dread like she had never known filled her soul. She knew what was happening, but did not want to say it aloud and make it real.

'*Are* the stars falling?' asked Silver. His eyes were wide, his lips pulled back from his teeth. His crooked old body was crouched low and trembling.

'He built a beacon,' Rana said. 'I tried to stop it, but I was too late.' Peering at the frightened wolves around her, she saw Karla among them, looking upwards, her mouth grim.

'It's happening,' Karla said. 'The old stories are coming true.'

The stars were falling. But as they came closer, they were not stars, but balls of flame, trailing from the jaws of creatures on dark wings.

CHAPTER 31

They dropped from the sky like gigantic diabolical bats, the first landing on top of the Victory Tower, buckling the monument with its weight. The wolves in the canyon below looked up in horror as the symbol of their superiority shattered. The dragon stretched out a long neck and bellowed, sending a fiery plume of breath into the dark night sky.

Many wolves in the canyon turned to flee as more dragons arrived, some landing on the crags of Howling Rock above them, others circling beneath the risen moon. And they brought fire, a force against which wolves were helpless—a power that filled their nightmares with visions of burning forests.

The dragons circled lower and lower. Their heads turned this way and that, studying the land of the wolves with cold, calculating eyes. The great rock tower was obviously the home of their foe. Around it, dozens of wolves swarmed, gaping upwards. Nearby was a great orchard, clearly an important resource.

One dragon gave an eerie cry, and they all swooped low over the leafy heads of the wolf-apple trees. Jaws opened, and fiery breath ripped through the canopy; branches crackled and ignited. The pack could only watch helplessly as the dragons flew round and round, destroying their precious source of food with every breath. Flames rose high into the night, and a pall of smoke began to cover the land.

While others ran in all directions, Rana stood at the main entrance to Howling Rock, staring upwards, taking in every detail. This was it, the day when legends became real. Seeing these fearsome creatures made her realise just how much younger Lyricon was. Their scaly bodies were considerably larger, the spines along their backs sharper, their eyes more terrible. Their savage jaws crackled with flame. When they spread their wings, the dragons seemed immense. They were fearsome creations, relics of the

Far-off Time. Compared to these invaders, Lyricon was just a cub.

And he might be the pack's only hope. Should she go back up to the Dragon Cave and try talking to him again? He had summoned the dragons, so maybe he could talk to them—tell them about the wolves who had cared for him, brought him fish, saved his life. There was no need to fight. With a deep breath, she turned towards the entrance and took one step inside.

Suddenly, she felt herself being dragged away by the scruff of her neck. She cried out but was not released until she had been pulled well away from the great rock. It was Darkmane. He had carried her back towards the edge of the pine forest, where many wolves were gathering.

'Are you crazy?' he growled. 'We need you alive. You're the only one who understands these things!'

Rana noticed that Karla was among the group.

'I hear they sent you away,' said the old she-wolf. 'You chose a heck of a time to come back.'

'If I had returned earlier, this might not have happened,' Rana replied. She looked helplessly back at Howling Rock. One of the invaders had landed at the main entrance, where she'd just been standing.

'I will rally our best warriors,' roared Sly, peering into the smoky haze for his scattered forces. 'We will never give up our home!'

Another dragon had landed and was looking curiously at the small caves tucked around the side of the Rock.

'Not the dens!' cried Karla. 'Come on!'

The dragon extended its long neck towards the den entrances. As it began to look inside, Gripper pounced on its tail and gave a savage bite at its thinnest point, just before the spike at its end. The dragon cried out and whirled around, sending Gripper sprawling in the dirt.

As the dragon advanced on Gripper, Sly and Darkmane appeared with the warriors they had mustered. They leapt on their enemy's back, snapping at its flanks and harrying it, the way they would tackle a grizzly. This was the first enemy to place itself within claw's reach and they would make it pay. The great creature twisted and roared, flinging them aside with a beat of its wings and a whip of its tail.

Taking advantage of the distraction, Rana and Karla dashed into the dens. Parents crouched protectively over whimpering cubs. Injured and elderly warriors stood guard on shaky legs. Everywolf was afraid. Smoke was beginning to creep through the cave openings.

'We need to get them out of here now!' said Karla. The little cubs looked terrified.

'Don't worry,' the old she-wolf said softly, nuzzling Scruff and Fluff. 'You're going to be taken somewhere safe.' She paused, uncertain. Where could wolves be safe from such an attack?

'We're going to a magic land,' Rana said suddenly. Karla gave her a curious look.

'Yes, a wonderful place like a giant den,' Rana continued. 'It's full of flowers, birdsong, plump turkeys to eat, and it has a secret sun all of its own.'

Rana and Karla peered outside. The smoke was spreading rapidly, and it was getting hard to see what was going on. The dragon Gripper had attacked was hovering in the sky, and Sly and Darkmane's warriors stood at bay, unsure of their next move.

Yes, thought Rana to herself. *Dragons may be more powerful, but we wolves can be trickier.* She quickly told Karla and Fenn what she had in mind.

'Insane!' said Fenn. 'But brilliant. Let's do it.'

'In all my years, I have never heard anything like it,' said Karla. 'But I see something in your eyes. Fera is with you.'

'First, I need to talk to Darkmane,' said Rana.

'Talk to me, then,' said Darkmane, who had appeared behind her. 'These dragons can fly out of reach whenever we fight back. Then they can burn us from the sky. We cannot fight them—not now. We need a plan. We must protect the pack.'

Rana explained her plan, the older wolf listening wide-eyed.

'I'll need a distraction to get everyone out of the dens,' said Rana. 'Hopefully, all the smoke will give us enough cover, but with the full moon tonight—and all the dragonfire—we need all the help we can get.'

'No problem,' said Darkmane. 'I can send Hunter and some of the runners out to Thorny Gap to lead some of our flying foes away on a wild goose chase. Better than that, Sly is itching for a fight. He wants to rush the main entrance, attack the dragon on guard and show them they can be hurt. If that doesn't get their attention nothing will. The warriors will support him, but I'll try to keep them from harm—if I can!'

Ayala, Lupey and Fenn helped gather everyone together into the largest den and calm them down. Rana peeked outside again. The largest dragon, the one that had arrived first, had started to crawl down Howling Rock slowly, clinging to the crags with splayed claws like an enormous lizard. It stopped by the narrow dark holes that formed the windows of Lyricon's chamber. Peering inside, it opened its huge jaws and let out a victorious cry.

He's been found, she thought. *They'll see we had him prisoner. What now? Will they hunt and destroy us all?*

She looked around at the wolves of all seven packs now readying themselves to flee: Starlight, Horizon, Sundown, Stalker, Snowfoot, Lightning and Cowbird. Young and old, all were trembling, exchanging anxious nuzzles. These were her people and she loved them, even the difficult and misguided.

I can't let them die.

'I'll take over now.' A querulous voice came from behind her. Silver had appeared out of the murk, a strange look in his eyes. His ears were flat, his tail down, his body quivering. 'I'll be in charge of the hiding. Everyone must go back into their designated dens, right away.'

'We can't stay here,' said Rana. 'The dragons are burning everything. We have to get away while they are distracted—live to fight another day.'

'Get away?' The old wolf gave a cracked laugh. 'Who can get away from such creatures of magic? Now, be silent, yearling. Remember, you are a traitor and an exile!'

'She is not a traitor, you old fool!' growled Karla. 'She tried to warn you about Lyricon, and you drove her out! Thank Fera she is now back. If anywolf here is a traitor, you are! All you cared about was more power! Well, here's your power now,' she said, pointing with her snout at the fiery chaos outside. 'Take a good look at it.'

Silver's eyelids were fluttering oddly. 'And you are a dangerous rebel!' he snarled. 'I will see that you are driven out of the pack too!'

'So, there you are!' A grim snarl interrupted them. Sly was approaching. There was a moment of silence as he walked towards Silver, his fur bristling and his teeth bared.

'Come on, you old coward, the Great Pack needs you! We are fighting for our home! What will they say of the Seven Fangs if so-called heroes like you stay quivering here with the cubs?'

Sly shoved Silver out of the cave. The old wolf tried to protest, but stopped when he saw Darkmane and the warriors staring at him.

'We fight for our lives!' roared Darkmane. The warriors howled in response. Silver had a desperate look in his eyes, but with all the wolves in full cry all around him, he could not back down. Reluctantly, he joined the throng.

Rana looked with anxious eyes towards her father, but instead met another gaze. Karla stood before her with a sad expression.

'Goodbye, little one,' said the old she-wolf.

Rana's eyes were wide. 'Y-you're going too?'

'Ever since the packs united, I've lived in dread that the dragons would return, just like in the time of Frost and the Sunrise pack. Now they are here, I have a chance to face my nightmare and find peace.'

'But we need you. The cubs all need you. They're afraid, and you're their storyteller. I—'

'Hush, child. You are the storyteller now. Take them to the safe, magical place in your story. Maybe one day, I'll find you there. Go with Fera!'

'With Fera!' echoed Rana, a sob in her voice.

And her friend was gone, lost in a whirl of fur as the wolves howled into battle.

They had to move quickly. Rana remembered how in the Forbidden Tale the dragons had easily spotted the wolves from above, because the Sunrise pack had made the mistake of only using well-worn paths. With the nearest dragons distracted by the warrior attack and Hunter's runners, Rana and Ayala led their group to the mouth of the den. Rana gestured with her snout towards the edge of the pine forest.

'All of you—get under cover over there. Run as fast as you can!'

Hidden by the smoke from the burning orchard, the wolves raced across the canyon into the trees. Rana held her breath watching the old and injured wolves bring up the rear, some helping parents with larger litters by carrying the littlest cubs by the scruff of the neck. A few mothers with cubs too big to carry trotted more slowly to accompany their young every step of the way.

Soon, the escaping wolves were gathered under the spreading branches on the edge of the great forest.

'So far, so good,' Rana said. 'Now, we'll avoid the

main trail. Follow me.' She made the wolves weave through the sprawling ferns, low shrubs and knots of grass of the forest floor.

Ayala, Lightfoot and Fenn were running up and down the line of fleeing wolves to keep them moving—and check that nowolf was left behind. Yearlings who were too young to be considered warriors had also joined the exodus.

'Need any help?' Rana was pleased to see Fenn appear by her side. 'Dad told me to come and take care of you,' he said. 'I wanted to fight the dragons, of course, but he said your safety was more important. He's weird.'

Rana smiled. 'Thanks, Fenn. I feel a lot safer now.'

'I never liked that dragon,' said Riki, padding along next to Ela. 'Big green show-off.'

'Totally,' agreed Ela. 'I am *so* over dragons. And just look at the soot in my fur.'

'It's lucky Rana came back to save us,' Riki added. 'I always liked her.'

'Me too,' said Ela. 'I mean, we're practically best friends. But don't talk too soon about being safe. We're not out of this yet.'

The snaking column of wolves of all ages and sizes made slow progress through the underbrush. Lupey trotted up to speak to Rana.

'We'll get nowhere fast like this,' he said. 'I suppose you know the story of *Hopeless Hare and the Long Shortcut*?'

'This is not the time for a story, Lupey!' said Rana. 'I'm keeping us out of sight.' Suddenly, she stopped. 'Wait—maybe there is a shortcut we could use . . .'

'The old deer track,' said Lupey. 'It's not too far from here.'

'It's so overgrown the dragons won't see it from above, but enough of a trail for us to speed up a bit. It's worth a try!'

Rana and Lupey led the wolves out of the thick scrub, and into a tract of ancient forest. The old deer path there was like an obstacle course, with fallen trees and hoary creepers hanging down everywhere.

'Now, we can get moving,' Rana said. 'We're making for Thunder Edge. Pass it back along the line.'

The excited murmur of Thunder Edge travelled back among the following wolves. Ayala came rushing up to join her daughter.

'Are you sure about this?' she said. 'What about the creek?'

Peering ahead, Rana pulled a face. 'I kind of forgot about the creek.' She sighed.

They called the wolves to a halt under the thick grove of great white oaks. Ahead, they could see the rushing brook glimmering in the moonlight. Crossing it would leave them briefly exposed to the sky. As they looked up, a dragon flew overhead, gazing this way and that.

'Go now!' said Lightfoot, the moment it had passed. 'Judging from its flight speed, that monster will take ages to circle back.'

'Move!' Rana shouted.

The great line of wolves plunged into the chilly waters. Riki yelped at the cold, and was shushed by Ela. The creek was deeper than it appeared, and some cubs had to be carried by the scruff of their necks again. In no time at all, they were clambering out the other side, dripping and cold.

'Where are we going?' said Lightfoot, running up to join Rana. 'Are you really heading for Thunder Edge? Big mistake. There's zero cover after there.

It's not like nipping across a creek. The dragons will hunt us down for sure.'

'We won't need cover after Thunder Edge,' said Rana.

Lightfoot scratched his brow with a forepaw. 'Are you a wizard now, Rana?'

'She is,' said Fenn. 'And she is going to make us disappear.'

CHAPTER 32

'Retreat!' cried Darkmane. Another blast of flame scattered the wolves and sent Haze yelping with a scorched tail. She was one of the lucky ones. Two from Horizon pack had vanished in a blast of fire and smoke, never to be seen again. The warriors had been trying to force their way back into Howling Rock without success.

'We gain nothing from this,' said Darkmane, as the warriors regrouped, readying themselves for another attack on the seemingly immovable dragon guarding the main entrance. 'Except to prove to them that they are superior.' He licked a singed paw, ruefully.

'But we cannot accept defeat!' growled Sly.

'We have not been defeated,' said Karla, with a grim smile. 'This attack has served its purpose.'

'What do you mean?'

'The rest of the pack is escaping. There is a plan.'

'Escaping?' A shrill laugh came from Silver. 'There is no escape, you fools. You told me to look upon their power, Karla—and I have. It is our destiny.'

'What is our destiny?' Karla asked.

'You shall see . . .'

Silver stepped forward from the horde of warriors—the bruised, the scorched, the exhausted. He walked with his delicate tread, straight towards the dragon. The others were shocked to see him lower his head and tail, crouching in submission.

'I am Silver of the Great Pack,' he cried. 'We have seen your power, Lord Dragon, and bow before you. Let me be your chief servant in this humble realm. Restore our home to us, and I will see that all wolves obey your will!'

'Chief servant?' roared Sly. 'I will kill him!'

'No,' cried Darkmane, holding Sly back. Darkmane had seen what was coming. The dragon lowered its head towards Silver, and with one breath, blasted the old wolf into ashes. There was a hush as the dark creature reared over the smoky patch where Silver had once stood to address the group of warriors.

'Restore your home?' The dragon laughed. 'I am Alakor of Ormeria. This is *my* home now. Chief servant? I need nowolf to help me rule.' Alakor's head swayed slowly from side to side on a long neck. 'You imprisoned my brother!' he roared. 'A noble spirit now barely alive. Your kind will be punished with devastating effect. Any who survive will be as scattered and lowly as the merest creatures of the hedgerow.'

A blast of fire drove the wolves further back, searing the fur of the front rank of warriors.

'Don't you understand? We have been toying with you,' sneered Alakor. 'Assessing your strength before we strike. You may have been mighty among this realm of rabbits and deer, but you are nothing to us dragons.' He paused to sniff the air. 'I know there are more of you, fleeing even now. They will be cut down too. Your land is ours now, your lives forfeit.'

In the night sky, more dragons could be seen descending.

'Run,' Darkmane ordered, addressing the warrior

group. His message was urgent but his voice was calm and without fear. 'Each wolf must run in a different direction. That way, some may survive.'

'Go it alone for one moon,' said Karla. 'Then listen for the ancient Howl of Gathering on the night winds. Fera will guide you. Now go!'

As the new squadron of dragons brought a rain of fire, the warriors of the Great Pack disappeared into the smoke.

CHAPTER 33

'Well?' said Alakor. 'What of the rest of the pack?' The dragon had flown back to the top of Howling Rock to survey the devastation around him. The spire of stone stood like a lonely island in a sea of smoke and flame. Beyond the burning orchard, the near edge of the pine forest was now being torched.

'No sign of them,' said Garalon, who had landed by Alakor's side.

'What? How can you lose a whole wolf pack?'

'Well, they are quite small,' said Garalon, his tail curling a little. 'And it *is* night-time.'

'Pathetic!' snarled Alakor. 'They are obviously in

this forest somewhere. Just burn the whole thing. Take the entire second squadron. This tower is conquered now. I will guard it with the first squadron, and stay with Lyricon.'

'How is the prince?'

'He was unconscious when I found him. The magic he created to summon us here was an extraordinary feat, and it took its toll.'

'You must be very anxious—'

'Your concern is noted, Garalon. He has suffered much but will survive. Now go and roast some wolf!'

With a beat of his wings, Garalon launched into the air, summoning his team with a vertical plume of fire.

'You're all on Seek-and-destroy now,' he said to the group hovering before him. 'Fly two leagues out from here—then circle back in. Kill any wolves on sight. The vermin must not get through our net.'

CHAPTER 34

'This is not good,' said Fenn, looking up. He, Rana and Ayala peered up through the leaves, watching the new tactics of the dragons. They were drawing closer and closer, flying in low, slow circles.

'They will spot us for sure,' said Lightfoot. 'I knew we went the wrong way.'

'We only need to reach Thunder Edge,' said Rana. 'And we're nearly there. Chase everyone along for the final push!'

Keeping to the deepest shadows, the wolves leapt and scrambled up to the lonely ridge of ancient trees. Much of the ground here was boggy from a nearby spring, slowing their progress.

'We had better be careful,' said Lightfoot. 'There's a dangerous hole up here, bottomless, they say. All the runners know about it.'

'Oh really?' said Fenn. 'Don't be so sure.'

'Look,' said Rana. 'There it is.'

Rising above the other trees ahead was a single, lightning-scorched pine, half of its branches blackened and split.

'Get down!' Lightfoot cried suddenly.

In the sky, a searching dragon drew dangerously close. It flew so low they could see every wrinkle on its long stomach, the pattern of glinting scales on its limbs. Its wings seemed to glow as the moonlight shone through the translucent skin. As soon as it passed, Rana called the whole line of wolves together.

'The moon is strong tonight, and we are about to break cover,' she said. 'But dragons have worse night vision than we do. I want you all, especially those with light-coloured fur, to roll in the black mud of the bog back there. Get yourselves properly stinky dirty.'

'Nice thinking,' said Lupey.

Lightfoot frowned. 'If we just run quickly . . .' he began.

'No, the mud!' insisted Rana. 'If a dragon looks down as we break cover, it may just see a moving darkness and pass us off as a shadow.'

'In the muck, quick!' barked Ayala. The wolves obeyed.

Ela and Riki were the last to jump in. 'Maybe Rana really is mad,' said Riki, peering at the mud and slime.

'Yep.' Ela sighed. 'But hey, you have to run with the pack.' She rolled over in the dank, dark bog.

'Think of it as beauty treatment,' said Fenn, urging them to hurry up. Soon, all were ready. The muddy wolves gathered on the edge of the forest, under the tree shadows.

'Looking good,' said Rana, eyeing them with approval. She shook her head to get the muddy fur out of her eyes. 'Now, when I give the signal, follow us. Do as we say, and you will be safe.'

She and Fenn broke cover and ran to the edge of a great crack in the ground. They were staring into the black pit of Thunder Edge. They could hear the underground stream rushing below.

'Are you sure the water is deep enough?' Fenn asked.

Rana nodded. 'I'll stake my life on it,' she said.

'Actually,' said Lightfoot, who had joined them, 'you are staking all our lives on it.'

'Yes, I am,' said Rana. 'I'll go first.'

'No, I'll go first,' said Fenn. 'We need you up here to convince the others. Everywolf listens to you.'

And with that, he leapt into the pit. There was a moment of silence, then a rather quiet splash. Rana and Lightfoot exchanged a look.

'The dragon is on its way back,' said Lupey.

The darkness of the pit was horribly silent. Waiting for a sign of life seemed to go on forever. Then, a cry. 'I'm OK!' yelped Fenn. 'It worked. Sorry, I swallowed some water.'

'Go!' howled Rana.

One by one, the wolves leapt into the pit.

CHAPTER 35

A bedraggled Rana clambered out of the pool and shook her fur. All around her, soggy wolves were bobbing in the dark waters. Parents were pulling their young to safety with firm but gentle jaws.

'Well, if I can survive that at my age, I think I can survive anything,' said Lupey, squatting on a rock, his grey fur a soggy mess.

As they scrambled up onto the rocks, wolves young and old gazed in relief—and disbelief—at the great watery cavern that hid them from the perils above. Mothers nuzzled their cubs, and friends exchanged smiles as they emerged dripping onto the path at the side.

'Where are we?' asked Lightfoot.

'On the secret path to Ungoria,' said Fenn. 'You can get down to it this way, but not back out again. Luckily, that's not our problem now.'

'What's an "Ungoria"?'

'Somewhere even you runners haven't been,' said Fenn. 'I don't think you'll be disappointed.'

'Brilliant,' said Riki. 'Can we have a rest now?'

'No,' said Rana. 'We have to get moving as quickly and quietly as possible, so the dragons have no chance of hearing, smelling or guessing where we have gone.'

It was good to see that all the wolves had made the leap safe and sound, but Rana's heart went out to all the ones left behind, fighting and running. Was her father attacking a dragon right now? Would Karla be alright? And what had happened to Lyricon? Had he really meant to bring down such disaster on them all?

'Do you think they will guess we went down here?' asked Ela anxiously.

'I don't think so,' said Rana. 'They don't know our land at all. From above, this just looks like a narrow, dangerous pit. From the air, all they'll see is a crack or shadow among the rocks, if that. There are some disadvantages to staying high up, on the wing.'

They peered up at the small circle of sky, but there was no sign of the dragon overhead.

'I was tracking its movements just before I dived,' said Lightfoot, who had been the last to jump. 'I think it's already moved further inwards. You *are* a wizard, Rana.'

Ayala looked up the dark tunnel ahead. She sniffed the chilly night air. 'Is there really a wonderful land down here?' she asked doubtfully. 'Or was that just to comfort the cubs?'

Rana smiled. 'Did you think I was just telling stories? Wait and see.'

CHAPTER 36

The sun rose to a scene of stark destruction. Howling Rock belonged to the dragons now. Every passage and cave had been scoured with fire. In the hollows where the guards had stood watch, all grass, bush or greenery of any kind had been burnt away.

Alakor was perched on top of the Rock, keenly awaiting news from the second squadron. The rising sun silhouetted every spike and barb of his thorny hide, and the long sinuous tail that dangled over the edge. In the distance, he could see thick smoke rising up among the pines. Not far off, Garalon was returning. The dawn light revealed a grim smile upon Alakor's face.

Garalon landed next to his commander with a lightness that belied his great size.

'I see the distant flames. They are all destroyed?' said Alakor. 'You took your time about it.'

'My Lord,' Garalon said. 'Those flames were just my team trying to scare some of these dratted creatures out from wherever they are hiding. We didn't find a thing. They must have some art or secret of which we do not know.'

Alakor was ominously silent.

'We will continue to search, of course,' Garalon said, scanning the horizon to avoid the gaze of his superior.

'Outwitted by a bunch of mangy dogs,' said Alakor. 'It will look well on your record.'

Garalon sought to change the subject. 'My Lord, what is the latest news of Prince Lyricon? You know how he is loved among the squadrons.'

Alakor did not look happy. 'He recovers, but is raving madly. Keeps saying something about us sparing the wolves. I suppose he means we are *not* to spare them. His captivity has broken his wits, no doubt.'

Garalon took to the air again. 'I shall not rest until his wish is fulfilled.'

CHAPTER 37

In later years, many tales were told of that escape. Tales of a great trek along an underground river, Rana at their head, only a yearling, yet chosen by Fera to bring hope to her pack. It was slow going with the very young and the very old, the wounded and those affected by smoke. Yet they all gradually made their way along the dark passage.

There were rockfalls to climb, stepping stones to leap across, roots to clamber over and stalactites to duck under and around. As the wolves' eyes grew more accustomed to the gloom, there were giant bats to gape at, and centipedes scuttling into corners. In the dark waters, long snakes were seen, some glimmering with luminous scales. Among the many side-pools, cubs were scolded for holding up the group by chasing exotic frogs.

Many wolves had a loved one—a mother or father, brother, sister or friend—who had been left behind, facing the dragons. Those who had escaped had no way of knowing what had happened back at Howling Rock, who had survived to flee into the secret ways of Hunter's Reach, and who, perhaps, would never be seen again.

Regardless of their worries, there were none who failed to appreciate the miracle of their escape. To leave behind the sky of fire and fear and plunge into a secret tunnel of quiet and safety really did feel like a blessing from Fera. Many times, Rana heard her own name whispered by her fellow travellers, from the old of Snowfoot pack to the young of the Cowbird clans, talking about her and Fenn in hushed tones.

As the wolves' sensitive noses scented the lush forest of Ungoria ahead, a kind of cautious hope spread through the throng. It felt like they were about to step into an impossible dream of summertime. And there were none who were not filled with wonder when they finally emerged, wide-eyed, into the fair underground realm. Owing to a twist in the tunnel, when Ungoria arrived it came rather suddenly—a great doorway of light, dripping with tangled creepers, abundant with hanging fruit, alive with darting birds and meandering butterflies.

'Ungoria!' gasped Lightfoot, gazing across the strange and beautiful forest. He gave Rana an astonished look. 'And you found this place—right under our noses?'

The rest of the Great Pack evacuees were ahead of him. Already, families were finding places to rest under giant toadstools or on mossy banks, huddling together. Some were expressing their joy in a livelier way, bounding through the soft grass and bushy clover with the last drops of their energy before flopping down with a sigh. One bright scamp from Lightning Pack had already caught a dozy mouse and was showing it proudly to its siblings.

'What do we do now?' Lightfoot asked, looking at Rana.

As Lightfoot asked this question, Rana realised something. It wasn't just him—everywolf was looking at her. At first, she felt puzzled, a small part of her wanting to run away and hide from the attention.

Then she realised she could not run away. The little cubs believed in her now, and the older had faith that she was guided by Fera.

Perhaps looking after Lyricon had added to her reputation. Her connection with his magic, and the mystery of her exile, all made her a wolf others talked about and expected marvels from. After all, she had brought them through a night of perils to a strange subterranean paradise . . . In the process, she had somehow emerged as a kind of leader. As she gazed at her pack, words of hope came naturally to her.

'We are the children of Fera,' said Rana. 'As the First Wolf said, these lands are ours. No dragon will take them for long. We will drive them back into the shadows. The Great Pack will rise again!'